THE STATUS OF THE CHURCH IN AMERICAN CIVIL LAW AND CANON LAW

This dissertation was approved by the Reverend John J. McGrath, A.B., LL.B., J.C.D., as director, and by the Right Reverend Clement Bastnagel, J.C.D., and the Reverend Romaeus W. O'Brien, O.Carm., M.A., J.C.D., as readers.

THE CATHOLIC UNIVERSITY OF AMERICA
CANON LAW STUDIES
No. 446

The Status of the Church in American Civil Law and Canon Law

A DISSERTATION

SUBMITTED TO THE FACULTY OF THE SCHOOL OF CANON LAW OF THE CATHOLIC UNIVERSITY OF AMERICA IN PARTIAL FULFILLMENT OF THE REQUIREMENTS FOR THE DEGREE OF DOCTOR OF CANON LAW

BY
REVEREND THOMAS F. DONOVAN, A.B., J.C.L.
PRIEST OF THE DIOCESE OF BROOKLYN, N. Y.

THE CATHOLIC UNIVERSITY OF AMERICA PRESS
WASHINGTON, D. C.
1966

NIHIL OBSTAT:

Right Reverend Clement Bastnagel, J.C.D.
Censor Deputatus

20 March 1966

IMPRIMATUR:

Bryan Josephus McEntegart, D.D., LL.D.
Episcopus Bruklyniensis

Bruklyni, die 23 March 1966

Murray and Heister, Inc.
Washington, D. C.

Printed by
Times and News Publishing Co.
Gettysburg, Pa., U. S. A.

FOREWORD

John Fitzgerald Kennedy stated his political-religious credo during his campaign for the Presidency of the United States. While addressing a group of Protestant ministers Mr. Kennedy stated:

> I believe in an America where the separation of church and state is absolute—where no Catholic prelate would tell the President (should he be a Catholic) how to act, and no Protestant minister would tell his parishioners for whom to vote. . . . I believe in an America that is officially neither Catholic, Protestant nor Jewish—where no public official either requests or accepts instructions on public policy from the Pope, the National Council of Churches or any other ecclesiastical source—where no religious body seeks to impose its will directly or indirectly upon the general populace or the public acts of its officials—where religious liberty is so indivisible that an act against one church is treated as an act against all —. . . I do not speak for my church on public matters— and the church does not speak for me. . . . But if this election is decided on the basis that 40,000,000 Americans lost their chance of being President on the day they were baptized, then it is the whole nation that will be the losers in the eyes of Catholics and non-Catholics around the world, in the eyes of history, and in the eyes of our own people.

The necessity of making such a statement during a presidential campaign bespoke the wary attitude held by some citizens with reference to the nature and goals of the Roman Catholic Church in the United States. The present work is intended to juxtapose the nature of the Catholic Church and the juridical constructions of the Constitution of the United States of America. The work will examine the nature of religious liberty in this country as guaranteed by the Federal Constitution. It will emphasize the fact that the religious goals and teachings of the Catholic Church flow from its supernatural foundation. Further it will be seen that the

Constitution of the United States insures the Church its right to prosecute its own ends and protects it from governmental intrusions.

The writer wishes to express his sincere appreciation to the Most Reverend Bryan J. McEntegart, Arch-Bishop, Bishop of the Diocese of Brooklyn, for the opportunity to undertake graduate studies in Canon Law, and to the members of the Faculty of the School of Canon Law of the Catholic University of America for their ready and willing assistance during the course of these studies. A debt of gratitude is also due to the Reverend John J. McGrath, LL.B., J.C.D., for his gracious help and direction in the preparation and revision of this dissertation.

TABLE OF CONTENTS

TABLE OF CONTENTS (Continued)

TABLE OF CONTENTS (Continued)

CHAPTER I

Religious Freedom in the United States of America

SECTION 1. THE NATURE OF THE CONSTITUTION OF THE UNITED STATES OF AMERICA

Pope Leo XIII (1878-1903) wrote

> Man's natural instinct moves him to live in civil society, for he cannot, if dwelling apart, provide himself with the necessary requirements of life, nor procure the means of developing his mental and moral faculties. Hence, it is divinely ordained that he should lead his life—be it family, or civil—with his fellow men, amongst whom alone his several wants can be adequately supplied.[1]

To attain the variety of social wants men form primary and secondary societies, or as they are also known, necessary and voluntary societies. When the men of any geographic region organize themselves to secure the goods of social tranquillity and security, this society is called the body politic. The body politic is then that particularization of the family of man oriented in a specific region to the goals of political independence and freedom. The body politic creates institutions, grounded on principles of social justice, directed toward temporal and political peace. The institutions so established by the body politic are received under the name of the state.

In the United States of America, the institutions comprising the state are characterized by a triple division of responsibility: the legislative branch, the executive branch, and the judicial branch. Each division has its own proper powers. The men appointed to direct the operations of the political institutions are collectively

---

[1] Pope Leo XIII, Encyclical *Immortale Dei,* 1 November 1885—*Acta Sanctae Sedis* (Romae, 1865-1908), XVIII (1885), 160-180 (hereafter cited *ASS*); translation: *The Church Speaks to the Modern World,* ed. E. Gilson (Garden City, N. Y.. Image Books, 1954), p. 162.

known as the government. Since it is the body politic that appoints the directors of the institutions, one can say that a government changes or falls whereas the state remains.

The proper powers of each of the political institutions together with their administrators are detailed usually by a constitution. A constitution is a politically inspired and written compact delineating the spectrum of authority which the people, the body politic, desire to grant to the government.[2]

It is important to note that the citizens are the source and object of all governmental powers. The constitution is created at their behest. It is directed and ordered to their temporal needs. The constitution does not grant rights to the citizens. It is rather the citizens who grant rights to the central government. Chief Justice John Marshall (1755-1835) made this citizen founded nature of the Constitution of the United States quite clear in his decision of *McCullough v. Maryland.*[3] Chief Justice Marshall wrote:

> The government proceeds from the people; and is ordained and established in the name of the people. . . . The government of the Union . . . is emphatically and truly a government of the people. In form and in substance it emanates from them, its powers are granted by them, and are to be exercised directly on them for their benefit. . . .[4]

To insure the proper discharge of activities and ordering of the temporal needs of the state the American Constitution provides for:

1. the office and departments of the federal government together with the specific delineation of their respective powers;
2. the localization of the supreme power of the state;
3. the rights of the citizens and the establishment of remedies for the vindication of these rights;

---

[2] McLouglin, *The Constitution of the United States of America,* Catholic University of America School of Law Doctoral Thesis (Washington, D. C., Catholic University of America, no date given), 5.

[3] *McCullough v. Maryland,* 16 U.S. 316, 4 L. Ed. 579 (1819).

[4] *Loc. cit.*

4. the orderly and internal process of amending the constitution itself.[5]

The rights of the citizens in the federal compact are interwoven throughout the Preamble and Text and are commented on in the decisions of the judicial branch of the government. The Constitution thus created devised

> . . a system in which the authority of that government over the state and the individual would not be excessive. . . . [This system] was achieved by empowering the new government to make and execute laws on those subjects which affected the nation as a whole; the problem was resolved by establishing a complex system in which governmental authority was widely distributed and rights were specifically guaranteed. . . .[6]

To secure the guarantee of rights the Constitution was developed in conformity with three principles: constitutionalism, federalism and the separation of powers.

Constitutionalism is that basic theory whereby the exercise of governmental power must be both authorized and limited by undertakings arrived at in advance and consented to by those affected and given continuing validity by appropriate enforcement processes. Such a theory of operation was intended to stand as a bulwark against arbitrary employment of governmental power.[7]

Federalism is the constitutional system predicating the existence of two complete governmental systems within the same geographic region and operating in reference to the same group of subjects. The American manifestation of this legal rule gave birth to a complicated arrangement whereby the national government exercises certain enumerated powers, all others being reserved to the States respectively, or to the people. "Each government is

---

[5] Shoup, *The National Government of the American People* (Boston: Ginn and Company, 1948), pp. 35-36.

[6] Hirschfeld, *The Constitution and the Court, The Development of the Basic Law through Judicial Interpretation* (New York: Random House, 1962), p. 5 (hereafter cited as Hirschfeld).

[7] Pritchett, *The American Constitutional System* (New York: McGraw-Hill Book Company, Inc., 1963), p. 11 (hereafter cited as Pritchett).

supreme within its own sphere; neither is supreme within the sphere of the other."[8]

The principle of the separation of powers is the third legal foundation of the Constitution. The initial sentence of the Constitution's First Article places all legislative activity in the Congress. The first sentence of Articles Two and Three similarly vests executive and judicial power in the President and in the courts respectively. Through this apportionment of unique responsibility the resultant institutions of each branch of government operate as a check and balance on the other two bodies of government. This ". . . division was in accord with the goal of limited government and was intended to make abuse of official power less likely."[9]

Through the three principles: constitutionalism, federalism, and the separation of powers, a constitution was framed to protect the rights of each of the citizens. The Constitution then became the paramount law of the Union.[10]

The problems of an ever growing and developing society must necessarily seek their legal solutions in the perduring principles of the Federal Constitution. But, the Constitution does not offer an explicit answer regarding which of the federal institutions is empowered to rule on authentic constitutional interpretations. Alexander Hamilton (1757-1804) believed the judicial branch of government had the responsibility of authoritative interpretation.

> A Constitution is in fact and must be regarded by the judges as a fundamental law. It therefore belongs to them to ascertain its meaning, as well as the meaning of any particular act proceeding from the legislative body. If there should happen to be an irreconcilable

---

[8] Mason, Beany, *American Constitutional Law* (Englewood Cliffs, N. J.: Prentice Hall, Inc., 1954), p. 4.

[9] Pritchett, pp. 10-11.

[10] *Marbury v. Madison,* 5 U.S. 368, 2 L. Ed. 60 (1803): " . all those who have framed written constitutions contemplate them as forming the fundamental and paramount law of the nation. . . . This theory is essentially attached to a written constitution and is consequently to be considered by this court as one of the fundamental principles of our society."

> variance between the two, that which has the superior obligation and validity ought, of course, to be preferred to the statute, the intention of the people to the intention of their agents.[11]

Hamilton's viewpoint became the radical foundation for the doctrine of judicial review as exercised by the Supreme Court.[12]

Chief Justice Marshall translated Hamilton's political theory into judicial practice in the *Marbury v. Madison* case.[13] William Marbury made formal application to the Supreme Court for a writ of mandamus to compel James Madison (1751-1836), the Secretary of State, to transmit Marbury's appointment as a justice of the peace for the District of Columbia. Marbury had been appointed to one of the "midnight judgeships" created by the outgoing President, John Adams (1735-1826). He based his plea for Supreme Court action on the Judiciary Act of 1789. Chief Justice Marshall, speaking for the Court, denied the petition, holding that the Act of 1789 was unconstitutional. Chief Justice Marshall stated:

> It is emphatically the province and duty of the judicial department to say what the law is. . . . Those who apply the rule to particular cases, must of necessity, expound and interpret that rule. If two laws conflict with each other the courts must decide on the operation of each. . . . The judicial power of the United States is extended to all cases arising under the Constitution . . it is apparent, that the framers of the Constitution contemplated that instrument as a rule for the government of courts, as well as of the legislature. . . .[14]

---

[11] Hamilton, Madison, Jay, *The Federalist,* Earle ed. (New York: Random House, 1937), p. 506; Beard (*The Supreme Court and the Constitution* [New York: The Paisley Press, Inc., 1938], pp. 15-63) analyzes the mind of the framers of the Constitution. Beard concurs with Hamilton's view that the Supreme Court was intended to be the final arbiter.

[12] Hirschfeld, *Constitution,* p. 10; cf. Jackson, *The Struggle for Judicial Supremacy—A Study of a Crisis in American Power Politics* (New York: Alfred A. Knopf, 1914), p. 8.

[13] *Marbury v. Madison,* 5 U.S. 368, 2 L. Ed. 60.

[14] *Loc. cit.*

The enunciation of the practice of judicial review in the *Marbury v. Madison* case has become the perduring right of the Supreme Court to the present day.[15]

The doctrine of judicial review is of singular importance when attention is turned to the constitutional meaning of religion in the American system of government. The courts look not only to the text and context but also to the historical background and present day psychology to fix the proper meaning of the Constitution. These issues are met and wedded in judicial review. The law itself and the judicial interpretations of the Supreme Court will form the twofold source of the American appreciation of the place of religion in the legal structure of the United States of America.[16]

SECTION 2. RELIGION IN THE CONSTITUTION OF THE UNITED STATES

The only explicit reference to religion in the original text of the Constitution is located in the Sixth Article of the document. Clause three of the Sixth Article states:

> The Senators and Representatives before mentioned, the members of the several State Legislatures, and all executory and judicial officers, both of the United States and of the several States shall be bound by oath or affirmation to support this Constitution; but no religious test shall ever be required as a qualification to any office or public trust under the United States.[17]

The absence of a more explicit statement of religious liberty was not received with equanimity by the people. A hue and cry was raised by the various states demanding a specific inclusion of a statement of the guarantees of religious liberty and other civil

[15] For a detailed discussion of the historical antecedents and practice of judicial review in the United States, cf. Gilligan, *The Development of the Idea of Judicial Review,* Master's Thesis, Columbia University, January 1954, esp. pp. 4-5.

[16] Kauper, "The Supreme Court and the Rule of Law," *Michigan Law Review,* LIX (1960), 532.

[17] Corwin, *The Constitution of the United States of America, Analysis and Interpretation* (Washington, D. C.: United States Printing Office, 1952), p. 736 (hereafter cited *Constitution*).

liberties.[18] To secure the desired civil liberties one hundred twenty-four amendments were suggested by the states in their conventions to ratify the Constitution. After prolonged debate, seventeen proposals were accepted by the House of Representatives. Upon transmission to the Senate, the number of amendments was reduced to twelve, and ten of these were accepted by the various states. The ten amendments became the Bill of Rights.[19]

The religious clauses of the First Amendment were therefore a product of the citizens' demand for greater assurance of their individual liberties. The First Amendment pragmatically states in sixteen words:

> Congress shall make no law respecting an establishment of religion, or prohibiting the free exercise thereof. . . .[20]

There has been a great deal of controversy as to what the First Amendment meant to its framers. In the latter part of this work there will be a review of the judicial interpretations and decisions regarding the present meaning of the First Amendment. For the present, it can be noted that there were five historical reasons which led to the incorporation of the First Amendment's religious clauses. First, the country was composed of a large number of unbelievers for whom religion was of little practical importance. Secondly, the variegated number of denominations necessitated a non-preferential position for each religious persuasion. Economic acceptance that religious persecutions brought a decline in commerce was the third factor. The fourth reason rested on the ever-widening acceptance of freedom of religion coming from the mother country, England. Americans began to criticize their own views of religion when compared with

---

[18] For a detailed history of religious expressions in the colonies and confederated states after the revolution, cf. Antieau, Downey, Roberts, *Freedom from Federal Establishment* (Milwaukee: Bruce Publishing Company, 1964); Nessel, *First Amendment Freedoms, Papal Pronouncements and Concordat Practice,* The Catholic University of America Canon Law Studies, n. 142 (Washington, D. C.: The Catholic University of America Press, 1961), *passim.*

[19] Corwin, *Constitution,* p. 750.

[20] Corwin, *Constitution,* p. 757.

those held in England.[21] The fifth historical factor was founded on the very considerable gains made in terms of human decency. Men were animated by an increasing sensitivity to human pain and suffering. Religious persecutions were psychologically repugnant and opposed to temporal peace and tranquillity.[22]

The second half of the First Amendment's religious clauses effectively secured the goals of domestic order. The first clause, limiting the action of Congress, made possible the full unfettered expression of the individual citizen's religious beliefs. Through the sixteen words of the religious liberty clause of the First Amendment the framers of the Constitution effectively turned back the European concept formulated in the sixteenth century, namely, that the relationship between man and God was a matter for legitimate legislative action.[24]

SECTION 3. BINDING FORCE OF THE FREE EXERCISE CLAUSE

The ratification of the Constitution deprived the federal government of any competence to legislate concerning the affairs of religion as such. It must be noted that the First Amendment, together with the other nine amendments, was designed to place restraint upon only the national government. The powers of the individual states were not incumbered in any fashion by the Bill of Rights.[25] One of the five offered amendments rejected by the Senate[26] would have placed the same limitations on the States in reference to legislation on religious questions. The rejected amendment read:

> The equal rights of conscience, the freedom of speech or

---

[21] Murray, *We Hold These Truths* (New York: Sheed and Ward, 1960), p. 58.

[22] Kurland, *Religion and the Law* (Chicago: Aldine Publishing Company, 1961), pp. 16-17.

[23] Kurland, "Of Church and State and the Supreme Court," *The University of Chicago Law Review,* XXIX (1961), 4.

[24] Pfeffer, *The Liberties of an American* (Boston: Beacon Press, 1956), p. 33.

[25] Guthrie, *Lectures on the Fourteenth Article of Amendment to the Constitution of the United States* (Boston: Little, Brown and Company, 1898), p. 5.

[26] *Supra,* p. 7.

> of the press, and the right to trial by jury in criminal cases, shall not be infringed by any state.[27]

In retrospect the incorporation of this proposed amendment would have obviated many judicial altercations. As it was, the Supreme Court consistently ruled throughout the nineteenth century that the Bill of Rights did not restrain the powers of the various States. Chief Justice Marshall stated that the limitations of the Federal Constitution were not applicable to the various states in his decision in the case of *Barron v. Baltimore.*[28] The case was a test of the right of the City of Baltimore to institute conservation plans without reimbursing the losses sustained by businesses as a result of that program. The plaintiff charged that the action by the City of Baltimore constituted an infringement of his rights under the Fifth Amendment of the Federal Constitution. The Supreme Court sustained the City of Baltimore. Mr. Chief Justice Marshall's opinion stated in part

> The constitution was ordained and established by the people of the United States for themselves, for their own government, and not for the government of the individual states. Each state established a constitution for itself, and that constitution provided such limitations and restrictions on the powers of the particular government as its judgment dictated. . . . If these propositions be correct, the fifth amendment must be understood as restraining the power of the general government not as applicable to the states.[29]

The Barron decision set forth the judicial principles which have been followed to some extent to the present time. This is truly a "landmark decision." The non-applicability of the Bill of Rights to the various state governments and their constitutions sprang directly from the *Barron* ruling.

The case of *Permoldi v. First Municipality No. 1 of New*

[27] *Annals of Congress, The Debates and Proceedings in Congress of the United States, First to the Eighteenth Congress* (Washington, D. C.: Gales and Seaton, 1834), I, 755.

[28] *Barron v. Baltimore,* 32 U.S. 245, 8 L. Ed. 672 (1833).

[29] *Loc. cit.*

Orleans was heard twelve years after the *Barron* decision. The *Permoldi* suit tested the religious clauses of the First Amendment with reference to state limitations. Father Permoldi asserted that the City of New Orleans had violated his religious rights guaranteed by the First Amendment in that it had passed an ordinance regulating burial practices. Father Permoldi conducted a religious service in contravention of the statute. He was convicted by a local court and brought the case on appeal to the Supreme Court. He contended that in performing the religious service

> . . . he was warranted by the Constitution and the laws of the United States, which prevented the enactment of any law prohibiting the free exercise of any religion.[31]

Father Permoldi's conviction was sustained in the opinion delivered by Mr. Justice Catron (1786-1865).

> The Constitution makes no provisions for protecting the citizens of the respective states in their religious liberties; this is left to the state constitutions and laws; nor is there any inhibition imposed by the Constitution of the United States in this respect on the states.[32]

The *Permoldi* decision reaffirmed the fact that the civil and religious liberties found in the Bill of Rights did not apply to the various states and further than any intrusions by the states into these areas would not be impeded in the federal courts. This ruling held true until 1868.[33]

The most significant change in the position of religion in the United States came about quite accidentally. In the days following the Civil War, the Northern controlled Congress brought about the incorporation of three amendments to the Constitution, the Thirteenth, Fourteenth, and Fifteenth Amendments. These amend-

---

[30] *Permoldi v. First Municipality No. 1 of New Orleans,* 44 U.S. 561, 11 L. Ed. 739 (1845).

[31] *Loc. cit.*

[32] *Loc. cit.*

[33] Sutherland, "Establishment According to Engel," *Harvard Law Review,* LXXVI (1962), 28-29.

ments were specifically directed to bring the Southern states into conformity with Northern principles. The Fourteenth Amendment through its due process clause became the radical source of applying the First Amendment to all the states. The pertinent passage of this amendment states:

> All persons born or naturalized in the United States, and subject to the jurisdiction thereof, are citizens of the United States and of the State wherein they reside. No State shall make or enforce any law which shall abridge the privileges and immunities of citizens of the United States, nor shall any State deprive any person of life, liberty, or property, without due process of law; nor deny to any person within its jurisdiction the equal protection of the law.[34]

The Fourteenth Amendment was incorporated in the Constitution in 1868, but its meaningful impact was not realized immediately. The amendment was not understood at the time of its passage as a restriction on the state's power over religion. This statement is demonstrated in a December 1868 case heard before the Supreme Court of New Hampshire. In the case of *Hale v. Everett,*[35] an action to enjoin a minister from occupying the pulpit of the First Unitarian Church because of supposed heresy, there was no mention made of the newly adopted amendment. The court's opinion ran to eighty-three pages. The dissenting opinion was one hundred forty-three pages. The non-inclusion of any reference to Fourteenth Amendment in either long opinion negatively demonstrates that contemporary courts did not consider the First Amendment to be applied to the various states through the Fourteenth Amendment.

Another decision, *United States v. Cruikshank,*[36] heard some seven years later mirrored a similar unawareness that the First Amendment's freedoms were in any way affected by the passage of the Fourteenth Amendment. The case dealt with the First Amendment's provision regarding the right of assembly rather

---

[34] Corwin, *Constitution,* p. 963.

[35] *Hale v. Everett,* 53 N.H. 9, 16 Am. Rep. 82 (1868).

[36] *United States v. Cruikshank,* 92 U.S. 542, 23 L. Ed. 588 (1875).

than its religious clauses. Still, the opinion given by Chief Justice Waite (1816-1888) does reflect the Court's view of the First Amendment.

> The particular amendment now under consideration assumes the existence of the right of the people to assemble for lawful purposes, and protect it against encroachments by Congress. . . . For their protection in its enjoyment . . . the people must look to the States. The power for that purpose was originally placed there, and it has never been surrendered to the United States.[37]

Chief Justice Waite's opinion therefore saw no expansion of the liberties secured by the Bill of Rights to the various states. The rule of law remained essentially what it was in the *Barron* case[38] and in the *Permoldi*[39] case.

The year the Supreme Court ruled in the *Cruikshank* case Senator James Blaine (1830-1893) introduced a proposed amendment to the Federal Constitution. In part his resolution read:

> No state shall make a law respecting an establishment of religion or prohibiting the free exercise thereof. .[40]

The significance of the amendment for the instant discussion stems from two factors. A) The wording of the Blaine Amendment with respect to its religious clause is a restatement of the First Amendment of the Constitution of the United States. B) The Congress which was asked to consider the proposal contained twenty-three members of the Congress that had enacted the Fourteenth Amendment.[41] The introduced change to the Federal Constitution seemed to be

> . . . the logical sequel to the presidential message of Ulysses S. Grant (1822-1885) delivered to a joint session

[37] *Loc. cit.*

[38] *Barron v. Baltimore*, 32 U.S. 245, 8 L. Ed. 672.

[39] *Permoldi v. First Municipality No. 1 of New Orleans*, 44 U.S. 561, 11 L. Ed. 739.

[40] Fourth Congressional Record, 175, 205 (44th Congress, 1st Session, 1875); Meyer, "The Blaine Amendment and the Bill of Rights," *Harvard Law Review*, LXIV (1951), 939-945.

[41] O'Brien, *Mr. Justice Reed and the First Amendment* (Washington, D. C.: Georgetown University Press, 1958), p. 116.

> of Congress just one week earlier than the proposal of the amendment.[42]

If the legislators had recognized the impact of the Fourteenth Amendment on the respective states then they certainly would not have bothered to expend their valuable time in a discussion concerning the advisability of introducing Senator Blaine's amendment for the consideration of the states comprising the Union. The discussion of the proposal by Congressmen Randolph, Christiancy, Kernan, Whyte, Bogy, Eaton and Morton in its behalf then would have been needless. That there was a debate which finally ended with the abandonment of the amendment clearly indicates that no such incorporation of the First Amendment through the provisions of the Fourteenth Amendment was envisioned in the 1870's.[43]

The awareness of the impact of the Fourteenth Amendment on the Constitutional law of the United States took time to evolve. In 1907 the restraint on the states through the Fourteenth Amendment clearly was not evidenced when Mr. Justice Holmes (1841-1935) wrote

> We leave undecided whether there is to be found in the Fourteenth Amendment a prohibition similar to that in the First [regarding a limitation of free speech.][44]

The lack of any restraint on the powers of the states was more emphatically stressed in 1922 in *Prudential Insurance Co. of America v. Cheek.*[45] In that case Mr. Justice Pitney (1858-1924) expressed the opinion of the Supreme Court when he stated

> The Constitution of the United States imposes upon the States no obligation to confer upon those within their jurisdiction whether the right of free speech or the right

[42] Klinkhamer, "The Blaine Amendment of 1875; Private Motives for Political Action," *Catholic Historical Review,* XLII (1956), 15.

[43] O'Brien, *Mr. Justice Reed and the First Amendment,* p. 117.

[44] *Patterson v. Colorado,* 205 U.S. 454, 27 S. Ct. 556, 51 L. Ed. 879 (1907).

[45] *Prudential Insurance Co. of America v. Cheek,* 259 U.S. 530, 42 S. Ct. 516, 66 L. Ed. 1044 (1922).

> of silence. . . . As we have stated, neither the Fourteenth nor any other provision of the Constitution . . . imposes upon the States any restrictions about "freedom of speech" or the "liberty of silence."[46]

It is true that the two foregoing cases do not directly deal with the right of freedom of religion. But since the freedom of speech and the freedom of religion are both part of the same First Amendment the interpretation of the Supreme Court regarding one clause of the Amendment would certainly be applicable to the other provisions of the Amendment in question.

The Supreme Court changed its view regarding the impact of Fourteenth Amendment in 1925 when it heard the case of *Gitlow v. New York*.[47] The plaintiff in the case was convicted on a New York statute prohibiting the advocacy of criminal anarchy. The Supreme Court held:

> For the purposes we may and do presume that freedom of speech and of the press which are protected by the First Amendment from abridgement by Congress are among the fundamental rights and liberties protected by the due process clause of the Fourteenth Amendment from impairment by the States.[48]

In finding for the appellant, the due process clause of the Fourteenth Amendment was applied to the various states for the first time. For the first time the powers of the various states were limited in respect to the freedoms of the First Amendment, specifically the freedom of speech.

After their ruling in the *Gitlow* case the justices of the Supreme Court gradually specified the rights protected against state intrusions in virtue of the Fourteenth Amendment's due process clause. However, it must be noted that the religious clause of the First Amendment was not formally treated until 1940. In the absence of any judicial review of the religious freedom clauses of the First Amendment the respective states were theoretically free

---

[46] *Loc. cit.*

[47] *Gitlow v. New York*, 268 U.S. 652, 45 S. Ct. 625, 69 L. Ed. 1138 (1925)

[48] *Loc. cit.*

to enact laws limiting the free exercise of a citizen's religious beliefs and to establish a religion as the official sect of the state. In practice, all the states had guaranteed the freedom of religion. Massachusetts was the last state to disestablish a religion. It did so in 1836.[49]

The freedom of religion was constitutionally guaranteed against state enactments in 1940 with the decision of the Supreme Court in *Cantwell v. Connecticut.*[50] The *Cantwell* case was the first time the due process clause of the Fourteenth Amendment was specifically applied to the freedom of religion clauses of the First Amendment. Mr. Cantwell brought his case on appeal to the Supreme Court. He was convicted together with his two sons of violating statute number 6294 of the State of Connecticut. The statute prohibited the solicitation of funds within the state for any charitable, religious or philanthropic cause without a prior license. The penalty was a fine of not more than one hundred dollars or imprisonment for not more than thirty days. The Supreme Court found the law a violation of the due process clause. Mr. Justice Roberts (1875-1955) stated the Court's opinion:

> The fundamental concept of liberty embodied in that Amendment [Fourteenth] embraces the liberties guaranteed by the First Amendment. The First Amendment declares that Congress shall make no law respecting an establishment of religion or prohibiting the free exercise thereof. The Fourteenth Amendment has rendered the legislatures of the states as incompetent as Congress to enact such laws.[51]

The *Cantwell* decision filled the void in American jurisprudence regarding the constitutional guarantee for religious liberty. The

---

[49] Massachusetts Acts and Resolves, 1782-83, Chapter 23, at 65 (1782) as amended by Massachusetts Acts and Resolves 1790-1791, Chapter 58, at 353 (1791), repealed by Massachusetts Laws 1834-1836, Chapter IV, at 539 (1836).

[50] *Cantwell v. Connecticut,* 310 U.S. 296, 60 S. Ct. 980, 84 L. Ed. 1213 (1940).

[51] *Loc. cit.*

Supreme Court secured the inalienable right of each citizen to follow the dictates of his own conscience against all governmental intervention. The *Cantwell* doctrine, in fact, reflected the concept that the central government and the governments of the various states had only those powers the people wished to grant them. The people did not grant to any group of legislators the right to enact laws concerning the relation on the individual with his God. The Fourteenth Amendment when applied to the First Amendment re-emphasized the right of each man to worship God and this without the approval of the government. Brown seems to have overlooked this fundamental principle of the American constitutional government when he wrote:

> There is, then, in the United States, a conflict between Church and State in the matter of public and private law. But, in practice, this clash of theories is softened by the State's allowing Catholics the right to practice their religion without molestation. [52]

The United States Constitution guarantees the right to worship as a fundamental law because this is the will of the citizens who form the compact of the governed.

> We set up government by the consent of the governed, and the Bill of Rights denies those in power any legal opportunity to coerce that consent. . . . If there is any fixed star in our constitutional constellation, it is that no official, high or petty, can prescribe what shall be orthodox in politics, nationalism, religion or other matters of opinion or force citizens to confess by word or act their faith therein.[53]

---

[52] *The Canonical Juristic Personality with Special Reference to Its Status in the United States of America,* The Catholic University of America Canon Law Studies, n. 39 (Washington, D. C.: The Catholic University of America, 1927), p. 5 (hereafter cited Brown).

[53] *West Virginia State Board of Education v. Barnett,* 319 U.S. 624, 63 S. Ct. 1178, 87 L. Ed. 1628 (1943).

CHAPTER II

The Roman Catholic Church: Its Foundation, Nature and Institutions

SECTION 1. THE ROMAN CATHOLIC CHURCH HAS BEEN FOUNDED BY JESUS CHRIST

The Roman Catholic Church declares itself to be divinely established by Jesus Christ as the one religion to bring salvation to the world. Jesus Christ, the Son of God, established His Church on a group of disciples and used these men to bring His message of redemption to all mankind.[1] Christ completed the redemption of the world through His death on the Cross and His Resurrection.

> From this source, the Church equipped with the gifts of its founder and faithfully guarding His precepts of charity, humility and self sacrifice receives the mission to proclaim and spread among all peoples the kingdom of Christ and God and to be, on earth, the initial budding forth of that kingdom.[2]

The Church, then, founded by Jesus Christ is the supernatural means given by God to men for salvation.

It is supernatural because it was founded by the Son of God.[3] It is supernatural because the destiny of the Church is to unite the individual soul with God.[4] The Church is supernatural be-

---

[1] Matthew, 28: 18-19: "All power in heaven and on earth has been given to me. Go, therefore, and make disciples of all nations, baptizing them in the name of the Father, and of the Son, and of the Holy Spirit."

[2] *Constitutio Dogmatica De Ecclesia,* Sacrosanctum Oecumenicum Concilium Vaticanum Secundum (Romae: Typis Polyglottis Vaticanis, 1964), n. 5; Translation: National Catholic Welfare Conference, Washington, D. C. (hereafter cited *De Ecclesia*).

[3] Matthew, 16: 18: "And I say to thee, thou art Peter, and upon this rock will I build my Church."

[4] Romans, 5: 10-11: ". . . we were reconciled to God by the death of his Son, much more, having been reconciled, shall we be saved by his life. And

cause the means of sanctification, the sacraments, are supernatural.[5] The Body instituted by Christ to bring men the fruits of salvation is the Church which is "nothing less than the body of Christ made visible in the person of Christ."[6] The Roman Catholic Church then is a real but mystical union of the members with their Divine Head.

> As all the members of the human body though they are many form one body, so also the faithful in Christ . . . the head of this body is Christ . . . He is the head of the body which is the Church.[7]

SECTION 2. THE CHURCH IS A VISIBLE BODY

Christ did not leave the Church as an invisible union with each man attempting to fathom the will of God for his own particular salvation. Christ entrusted to men the function of bringing His message to mankind. The Apostles and the bishops, their successors, guide the efforts of all men toward salvation through the use of the sacraments.

> For the nurturing and constant growth of the People of God, Christ the Lord instituted in His Church a variety of ministries, which work for the good of the whole body. For those ministers, who are endowed with sacred power, serve their brethren, so that all who are of the People of God, and therefore enjoy a true Christian dignity,

---

not this only, but we exult also in God through our Lord Jesus Christ, through whom we have received reconciliation."

[5] Schroeder, *Canons and Decrees of the Council of Trent* (St. Louis, Mo.: B. Herder Book Co., 1941), pp. 51-52; 7 Session, can. 1: "If anyone says that the sacraments of the New Law were not all instituted by our Lord Jesus Christ or that there are more or less than seven, namely baptism, confirmation, Eucharist, penance, extreme unction, order and matrimony, or that anyone of the seven is not truly and intrinsically a sacrament, let him be anathema"; can. 7: "If anyone says that grace, so far as God's part is concerned is not imparted through the sacraments always and to all men even if they receive it rightly, but only sometimes and to some persons, let him be anathema."

[6] *De Ecclesia,* n. 5.

[7] *De Ecclesia,* n. 7.

working together toward a common goal freely and in an orderly way may arrive at salvation.[8]

Article 1. The Church Is Endowed With a Hierarchy

The task of sanctification is directed by the Pope and bishops who are the successors of the Apostles.[9] The bishops conjoined with the Supreme Pontiff and with their assisting priests form a twofold hierarchy. The term "hierarchy" means "sacred government."[10] The sacred government functions in both the order of sanctification of the members and in the field of the visible government of the Church. The former hierarchy is called the power of orders and the latter is called the power of jurisdiction.

Jurisdiction is founded on orders. But, there is a real distinction between the two hierarchies. The power of orders arises from a sacred rite,[11] whereas the power of jurisdiction stems from a canonical mission, i.e., "the grant of an ecclesiastical office by a competent ecclesiastical authority, made in accordance with the sacred canons."[12] The purpose of the two hierarchies is different. The power of orders looks to the sanctification of the member whereas the power of jurisdiction regards the proper ordering of the member within the Mystical Body of Christ.[13]

---

[8] *De Ecclesia,* n. 18.

[9] *De Ecclesia,* n. 20; *Codex Iuris Canonici, Pii X Pontifex Maximi iussi digestus, Benedicti Papae XV auctoritate promulgatus* (Romae: Typis Polyglottis Vaticanus, 1917), canon 218, § 1; canon 329, § 1 (hereafter cited *CIC.* can.).

[10] Bouscaren, Ellis, *Canon Law, A Text and Commentary* (2. ed., Milwaukee: The Bruce Publishing Company, 1951), p. 95 (hereafter cited Bouscaren).

[11] *CIC.*, can. 109; cf. *Codex Iuris Canonici Orientalis,* Pro Ecclesiis Orientalibus, adnotationibus fontium auctus, cura Pontificii Consilii Codici Iuris Canonici Orientalis redigendo, *Litterae Apostolicae Crebrae Allatae,* motu proprio datae, 22 febr. 1949; *Litterae Apostolicae Sollicitudinem Nostram,* motu proprio datae, 6 ian. 1950; *Litterae Apostolicae Postquam Apostolicis,* motu proprio datae, 9 febr. 1952; *Litterae Apostolicae Cleri Sanctitati,* motu proprio datae, 11 iun. 1957; *Cleri Sanctitati* canon 39 (hereafter cited as *Creb. Allat.*, can. ....; *Soll. Nostr.*, can. ....; *Postquam,* can. ....; *Cler. Sanc.*, can. ....).

[12] *CIC.*, can. 147, § 1; *Cler. Sanc.*, can. 88.

[13] Beste, *Introductio in Codicem* (5 ed., Neapoli: M. d'Auria, 1961), p. 173 (hereafter cited Beste).

The Church with its twofold hierarchy, then, looks to the proper ordering of the member to his eternal salvation. The direction is accomplished under the care of the divinely constituted office of bishops. The task here incumbent is to investigate the Church in its visible juridic structure rather than in its power of orders in order to perceive the forms it has established to accomplish its task, and to observe in what measure these institutions are received in American civil law.

Article 2. The Church Has a Structured Hierarchy

Inseparably conjoined with the theological reality of the Mystical Body is the structural organization within the Church. The structured system of authority is not a separate element within the Church. The visible hierarchy and the Mystical Body of Christ

> . . must never be considered as two things, but rather they form the complex reality which coalesces with a human and divine element.[14]

There could be envisioned a disjunctive relationship between the two elements forming the one reality if the two parts had a diversification of ends. But each hierarchy has the same ultimate goal.

> Christ, the one Moderator, established and continually sustains here on earth His holy Church, the community of faith, hope and charity, as an entity with visible delineation through which he communicated truth and grace to all.[15]

The structure of the power of jurisdiction was founded to serve the Body, not to be independent from the Body.

> For the nurturing and constant growth of the People of God, Christ the Lord instituted in His Church a variety of ministries, which work for the good of the whole

---

[14] *De Ecclesia,* n. 8.

[15] *Loc. cit.*

> Body . . . Jesus Christ, the eternal Shepherd, established His holy Church, having sent forth the apostles as He Himself had been sent by the Father, and He willed that their successors, namely the bishops, should be shepherds in His Church even to the consummation of the world. And in order that the episcopate itself might be one and undivided, He placed Blessed Peter over the other apostles, and instituted in him a permanent and visible source and foundation of unity of faith and communion.[16]

The Mystical Body of Christ is then not merely an association of spirit among the believers of the doctrine of Jesus. The act of faith by which a person freely accepts on the word of God the truth He has revealed incorporates the believer into a visible society which is the Church. This visible society is founded on a visible sign of unity, the Papacy.[17]

Article 3. Visible Institutions Established by the Church Can Be Changed

To effectively govern the Church in its power of jurisdiction the Church has evolved institutions in accordance with the needs of times and localities. In the first years of the Church its structures were rather simple. Jurisdiction was universal during the apostolic era. Each Apostle had worldwide authority. There was neither a fixing of areas of competence nor a need for any limitation as such. Although most of the Apostles confined their ministry to a definite region, there were instances of overlapping labors in identical areas. Paul, for example, went to Rome, although Peter was already there.[18]

Initially, the Apostles undertook all the works of the ministry. They preached, administered the sacraments, distributed alms, and managed the finances of the early Church. The increased number of converts expanded the burdens of the Apostles to such a degree that they could not adequately fulfill all their tasks. Peter

---

[16] *De Ecclesia,* n. 18.

[17] Matthew, 16: 18.

[18] Romans, 1: 10-11.

decided with the consent of the other Apostles to call upon the help of deacons, and placed in their charge the administration of the physical concerns of the Church.[19] Once a specific work was entrusted to the deacons, the structural development of the Church began to expand. The foundation of the diaconate and the commission to it of a work evidenced the reality that Christ did not specify the totality of the limits of each office. The Church was left to pursue its mandate according to the designs best determined by the men of each era.

With the death of the Apostles the particularization of the Church's structure was increased through the transfer of ecclesiastical jurisdictions to the successors of the Apostles. In an orderly transfer of authority from the Apostles to the bishops whom they had consecrated, the Church pursued its salvific mission. The new bishops faced problems of preaching and administering the sacraments to communicants in urban and rural areas that forced a new alteration in ecclesiastical structures. The people living in the rural areas, the *pagani,* could not be adequately cared for by priests traveling to their districts. Nor could they come to the towns with ease. Priests were assigned permanently to the rural districts, and eventually there was instituted in the Oriental Church the office of chorbishop to meet the needs of the *pagani.*

The chorbishops were dependent bishops deputed to work among the rural Christians by the city churches. They functioned under the direction of the city bishop. The I Council of Nicaea (325) evidenced their dependent nature in directing these chorbishops to annually exhibit their dependence on the city bishops.[20] The institute of chorbishop gradually fell into disfavor and was suppressed.[21] However the institute itself does witness the reality of a non-fixed structure in the Church. Apart from the divinely established offices of Pope and bishop the Church must meet its

---

[19] Acts, 6: 1-5.

[20] Labbeus, Cossartius, *Sacrosancta Concilia ad Regiam Editionem Exacta* (17 vols. in 18, Parisiis, 1671-74), II, 333.

[21] Kurtscheid, *Historia Iuris Canonici, Historia Institutorum* (2. ed., Romae: Officium Libri Catholici. 1951), pp. 59-60 (hereafter cited Kurtscheid).

problems with those structures that are best suited to bring the message of Christ to different cultures and times.

Another institution that grew, prospered and eventually fell into practical disuse was the office of the archdeacon. As was noted earlier, the deacons were constituted for the temporal necessities of the people.[22] Gradually, the deacons began to control the finances of the churches. They were in charge of the offerings.[23] From the general duties of the deacons emerged the office of archdeacon. Kurtscheid (1877-1941) maintained that the initial usage of the term is attributable to Optatus of Mileve, who employed the term as a designation for Cornelius, deacon.[24] The archdeacon was the bishop's aide. He was the vicar ruling the diocese. In particular, both the administration of the diocese's temporalities and the training of future clerics were entrusted to his charge. He was the agent of the bishop for the discipline of the diocese. He ruled the diocese during the bishop's absence.[25] The bishop often fulfilled his obligation of visiting the diocese through the archdeacon who was delegated for this purpose. During such visitations the archdeacon was empowered to make a final judgment in a variety of cases.[26]

The office of archdeacon shows an attempt, during a period of unsettled conditions, of the Church to meet the contingencies of the day. Archdeacons gradually were multiplied. Hinschius (1836-1898) stated that the see of Strassburg in 744 had multiplied the number of archdeacons,[27] and Van Epsen (1646-1728) recounted that Liège in 779 had as many as eight.[28] By the twelfth century the need for this particular form of a bishop's aide was no longer

---

[22] *Supra*, p. 21.

[23] *Constitutiones Apostolorum*, Liber II, canon 44-Labbeus-Cossartius, I, 282-283.

[24] Kurtscheid, I, 56.

[25] Kurtscheid, I, 161.

[26] II Council of Paris (614), canon 7—Bruns, *Canones Apostolorum et Conciliorum Saeculorum* IV-VIII (2 vols., Berolini, 1839), II, 214.

[27] *System des katholischen Kirchenrechts* (6 vols., Berlin: 1869-1897), II, p. 189, note 3.

[28] *Ius Ecclesiasticum Universum* (5 vols., Louvanii, 1753), Pars. I, Tom., XII, can. 1, n. 23, p. 76.

necessary. The office was reduced until now its principal task is to function during the rites of ordinations.[29]

The brief descriptions of the rise and extinction of the offices of chorbishops and archdeacons are presented with a view to exemplifying the reality that the Church's structure apart from the offices of pope and bishops undergoes alterations and evolution. The circumstances of place and time may require structural solutions that will not be fitting in other circumstances. However, throughout the evolutionary nature of the structures within the Church the reality of jurisdiction perdures as the means of properly ordering the faithful to their union with Christ, the head of the Church.

SECTION 3. THE CHURCH IS A TRUE SOCIETY

A society is a union of a plurality of men working together toward a common goal through the use of common means and directed by a legitimate authority.[30] The Church presents itself to the world as a society endowed with the qualifications of a true society. The Church is composed of a plurality of members, working for a common goal, salvation. Each of the members attempts to actualize the goal through the employment of common means. The use of the means is directed under lawful authority. The coalescence of these four elements within the Church gives proof to the fact that the Church is a true society, since a combination of these principles serves to constitute a properly defined society.

The multiplicity of members in the Catholic Church is an obvious fact. Catholic worship is offered to God in every area of the world. Men on every continent profess and publicly proclaim their allegiance to the Church's teachings. Christians embrace the faith for one goal, the sanctification of their souls, and to tender to their Father in heaven the purest form of worship of which they are capable.

The faithful actuate their goal of eternal salvation through the use of identical means of holiness. They profess the same belief.

---

[29] Fournier, *Les Officialites au Moyen Age* (Paris: 1880), pp. xxvii ff.

[30] Cappello, *Summa Iuris Publici Ecclesiastici* (6. ed., Romae: Aedes Universitatis Gregorianae, 1954), p. 83 (hereafter cited Cappello).

They are grouped together as a unified body through the partaking of the same sacraments, the same Sacrifice of the Mass and use of the sacramentals of the Church. They all profess and acknowledge the same source of spiritual teaching and governing authority, the bishops conjoined with the Supreme Pontiff.

Lastly, the faithful in embracing the Pontiff as the living interpreter of the unchanging words of Christ accept the divine commission to Peter and the Apostles and their successors as the legitimate source of government within the Mystical Body of Christ. In today's world various members of the international community give attestation to the Church as a society by having ambassadors and official representatives at the Vatican as an equal in the international society of nations.

SECTION 4. THE CHURCH IS A PUBLIC SOCIETY

In Our Lord's promise to be with His Church for all days are found the characteristics that make the Church to be truly a public institution.

The Church is concerned with all of the needs of men, irrespective of geographical or temporal consideration. It strives to bestow on all men the fulness of its teachings and benefits. Through its unceasing efforts, men have been led to perfection in the diverse elements of the natural society. Hospitals, schools, orphanages, and the works of charity are but a few examples of the Church's benefits to the civil community. Its repeated pronouncements on social peace and international questions of rights and justice constantly urge all levels of society to the goal of mutual respect and justice for all men. The goals of the Church today are the same as when Pope Leo XIII wrote the following.

> Neither must it be supposed that the solicitude of the Church is so preoccupied with the spiritual concerns of her children as to neglect their temporal and earthly interests. Her desire is that the poor, for example, should rise above poverty and wretchedness, and better their condition in life and for this she makes a strong endeavor. By the very fact that she calls men to virtue and forms them to its practice she promotes this in no slight degree. Christian morality, when adequately and

> completely practiced, leads of itself to temporal prosperity, for it merits the blessing of that God who is the source of all blessings; it powerfully restrains the greed of possession and the thirst for pleasure. . . . The common Mother of rich and poor has aroused everywhere the heroism of charity, and has established congregations of religious and many other useful institutions for help and mercy, so that hardly any kind of suffering could exist which has not afforded relief. At the present day many there are who, like the heathen of old, seek to blame and condemn the Church for such eminent charity. They would substitute in its stead a system of relief organized by the States. But no human expedients will ever make up for the devotedness and self-sacrifice of Christian charity. Charity, as a virtue, pertains to the Church; for virtue it is not, unless it be drawn from the Most Sacred Heart of Jesus Christ.[31]

SECTION 5. THE CHURCH IS A JURIDIC SOCIETY

The "household of God in the Spirit"[32] is not only a public society; it is a juridic society. A juridic society is one capable of imposing obligations on its members. Christ gave His apostles true jurisdiction over His Church when He said:

> Amen, I say to you, whatever you bind on earth shall be bound also in heaven, and whatever you loose on earth shall be loosed in heaven.[33]

The twofold power both of enacting laws and the relaxing of these same prescriptions indicates that Christ committed true authority to His Church. The Church was not to be limited merely to exhortation; it was given the right to bind its members internally and externally to specific modes of conduct.

The power of government was given by Christ without limitation. The Church's objective is to bring all men to the person of Christ. To assist it in its task

> . . . Jesus Christ gave to His Apostles unrestrained authority in regard to things sacred, together with the

[31] Encyclical, *Rerum Novarum—ASS*, XXIII (1890), 641-670; Translation: *The Church Speaks to the Modern World*, pp. 220-221.

[32] *De Ecclesia*, n. 6.

[33] Matthew, 16: 19.

> genuine and most true power of making laws, as also with the twofold right of judging, and of punishing, which flow from that power.[34]

If the Church did not have this power, it would lack the effective means of directing men toward Christ. The Church could not appropriately coordinate men on their path to salvation.

Article 1. The Church Has Legislative Power

The Church is a juridically perfect entity inasmuch as it possesses legislative power. Jesus Christ stated that His kingdom was not a temporal one when He stood before Pilate.

> If My kingdom were of this world, My followers would have fought that I might not be delivered to the Jews. But as it is, My kingdom is not from here.[35]

The spiritual kingdom of Christ is governed by its hierarchy in all the concerns of matters religious.

> It is to the Church that God has assigned the charge of seeing to, and legislating for, all that concerns religion; of teaching all nations; of spreading the Christian faith as widely as possible; in short, of administering freely and without hindrance in accordance with her own judgment, all matters that fall within her competence.[36]

Legislative power is defined as that part of the public authority of the society whereby the norms to be followed are: a) obligatory from the legitimately constituted source of authority, and b) directed for the common end of the community.[37] When Our Lord

---

[34] Leo XIII, Encyclical *Immortale Dei—ASS,* XVIII (1885), 165; *The Church Speaks to the Modern World,* p. 166.

[35] John, 18: 36.

[36] Leo XIII, *Immortale Dei; The Church Speaks to the Modern World,* p. 166.

[37] Conte a Coronata, *Institutiones Iuris Canonici* (4 vols., Vols. I-III, 4. ed., Vol. IV, 3. ed., Taurini: Marietti, 1950-1956), I, n. 26 (hereafter cited *Institutiones*).

stated His intention of conferring legislative power to Saint Peter and his successors the declaration was expressed in absolute terms.

> And I will give thee the keys of the kingdom of heaven; and whatever thou shalt bind on earth shall be bound in heaven, and whatever thou shalt loose on earth shall be loosed in heaven.[38]

It may seem obvious to remark that the promise was made to Peter. But legally, the recipient was not the secular society. The purpose of the authority was spiritual, to lead men to heaven. The civil authority has the temporal tranquillity of the members of its society as the ultimate goal of the public institutions. When Peter was told he was to receive legislative power over the kingdom of God on earth he obtained power free from any intrusions by secular authorities. It is important to recognize that the political culture of the day was not separate from the religious practices of the people. Yet from the beginning of the Church its hierarchy acted with complete independence of the secular powers. In the Council of Jerusalem (A.D. 49) the Apostles acted as the only ones commissioned with the legal responsibility of shepherding the people of God.[39]

Saint Peter in his Second Epistle clearly indicated that the Catholic faith is founded not on civil prescriptions but rather on Christ Jesus.

> For indeed His divine power has granted us all things pertaining to life and piety through the knowledge of Him who has called us by His own glory and power through which He has granted us the very great and precious promises, so that through them you may become partakers of the divine nature, having escaped from the corruption of that lust which is the world.[40]

The requirements of Church membership were independent of the prescriptions of Roman Law. All men were capable of join-

---

[38] Matthew, 16: 18.

[39] Acts, 15.

[40] II Peter, 1: 3-5.

ing the Church. The status of a man as either slave or free[41] was of no moment for one's life in the Church. The Church established its own laws regarding marriage. These laws were independent of Roman law.[42] The early Church legislated concerning cultural practices. Circumcision was not demanded of converts from paganism.[43] Legal prescriptions of the Old Law were set aside with reference to foods.[44]

The entire course of Church history details how the successors of the Apostles enacted laws for the spiritual good of the family of God. They did not have recourse to the civil society for its approval. The present Code of Canon Law declares formally that the Church is capable of legislating for matters of its own concerns and in fact obliges all Catholics to follow the laws enacted.

> The Roman Pontiff as the successor to the primacy of St. Peter has not only the prerogative of honor but also the supreme and full power of jurisdiction over the universal Church in matters of faith and morals as well as in those that pertain to the discipline and government of the Church throughout the world. The power extends over each and every Church, each and every pastor of souls, and over the faithful, and is independent of all human power.[45]

In local structures of the Church, i.e., the diocese, the bishop is the chief pastor of the souls entrusted to his care. The bishop as the successor of the Apostles has the duty of the government of the local church with legislative, judicial and coercive powers which must be exercised in conformity to the general laws of the Church. The bishops have the right to promulgate laws for their own territories.[46] The enactments detailing the rights and duties of Pope and bishop assert the legislative power of the Church. The Church uses this power for the salvation of all men.

---

[41] I Peter, 2: 13-25.
[42] I Corinthians, 7: 1-40.
[43] Acts, 10: 47-48.
[44] Acts, 15: 27-28.
[45] *CIC.*, can. 218; *Cler. Sanc.*, can. 162.
[46] *CIC.*, can. 335; *Cler. Sanc.*, can. 399, §§ 1, 2.

Article 2. The Church Has Judicial Power

A juridically perfect society must be capable of declaring the meaning, force and scope of laws enacted by the society. The society must be capable of settling the controversies arising within itself when there are conflicts between the members themselves and between the members and the society. This right of declaring the meaning of the laws and the settling of controversies is a consequence of the legislative powers of the society.

If the Church can legitimately enact laws, it is the only source endowed with the ability to determine the exact meaning of prescriptions. The Church could not claim to be a juridically perfect society if it had to invoke the judicial arm of civil society to settle ecclesiastical controversies or to rule on the meaning of Church prescriptions. In fact, the Church declares itself to the source of authentic interpretation of its own laws. It does not look beyond itself and its legal framework to find authentic interpretations of its enactments.

The assertion of its own competence in interpretation and adjudication of internal disputes has been made consistently from the time of the Church's foundation. Our Lord gave the Church the capacity to settle disputes among its members.

> But if thy brother sin against thee, go and show him his fault, between thee and him alone. If he listens to thee, thou hast won thy brother. But if he does not listen to thee, take with thee one or two more, so that on the word of two or three witnesses every word may be confirmed. And if he refuses to hear even the Church, let him be to thee as the heathen and the publican.[47]

Saint Paul reflected the same power given by Christ when he wrote:

> Dare any of you, having a matter against another, bring your case to be judged before the unjust and not before the saints? . . . If, therefore, you have cases about worldly matters to be judged, appoint those who are rated as nothing in the Church to judge.[48]

---

[47] Matthew, 18: 15-17.

[48] I Corinthians, 6: 1, 4.

In the same letter Saint Paul asserted his proper right to pass judgment when he condemned the man who had taken his father's wife as his own.[49]

The Code of Canon Law expressly states that the Church is the proper source of interpretation of its own laws.[50] The same universal law states that the meaning of laws is to be taken in accordance with the signification of the words in their text and context. However, if a doubt still remains concerning the meaning of the law, the source of interpretation is to be found in the parallel uses within the same body of law, the end of the law, the circumstances, and finally the mind of the legislator.[51] No mention is made of seeking interpretation from the secular arm of society. The Church alone is the sole authority in matters of its own laws.

In the section on legal procedures within the corpus of ecclesiastical legislation the Church holds itself to be exclusively competent in certain matters to the exclusion of all civil tribunals.

> The Church has the inherent and exclusive right to judge:
> 1. Cases which relate to spiritual matters, or to temporal matters annexed to spiritual.
> 2. Violations of ecclesiastical laws, and all other actions in which sin is implicated, insofar as the decision of the guilt and the infliction of ecclesiastical penalties are concerned.
> 3. All civil and criminal cases of persons who enjoy the privilege of the ecclesiastical forum, as defined by canons 120, 614 and 680.[52]

Not only does the Church vindicate itself as a juridically perfect society insofar as it claims all needed capacity for rendering judicial decisions within its own society, but it establishes which

---

[49] I Corinthians, 5: 3-5.

[50] *CIC.*, can. 17: "Laws are authentically interpreted by the legislator or his successor and by him to whom the power of interpreting has been entrusted by the same."

[51] *CIC.*, can. 18.

[52] *CIC.*, can. 1553, § 1; *Soll. Nostr.*, can. 2.

court enjoys competence over the various matters of judicial dispute.

The Church declares that the Holy See can be judged by no one.[53] The absolute inability of any power being superior to the Roman Pontiff precludes the possibility of a court having competence over the Pope.

> The Roman Pontiff, as the successor of Peter, is the perpetual and visible principle and foundation of unity of both the bishops and the faithful . . . the individual bishops represent each his own Church, but all of them together and with the Pope represent the entire Church in the bond of peace, love and unity.[54]

Since the Pope is the head of the Church and the bishops are part of the structural hierarchy only when in communion with the Pope as their head,[55] no person or group of persons are superior to the Pope and capable of judging him.[56]

Aside from the complete immunity of the Supreme Pontiff, the legal structure of the Church places certain classes of cases solely within the competence of the Holy Father. All ecclesiastical cases involving those who hold the highest rank of sovereignty in the civil sphere, their immediate families and those who succeed to their office are specifically reserved to the Pope. Suits involving legates of the Holy See and cardinals, and all criminal causes regarding bishops, are reserved to the person of the Pope.[57] To this category of actions may be added any case having an ecclesiastical nature in which the Holy Father desires to act as judge.[58] Contentious as opposed to criminal causes of residential bishops, and disputes involving moral persons in the Church who have no superior other than the Roman Pontiff are reserved to the tribunals of the Holy See.[59] Apart from these causes and such

---

[53] *CIC.*, can. 1556; *Soll. Nostr.*, can. 14.

[54] *De Ecclesia,* n. 23.

[55] " . if the latter (a bishop) refuses or denies apostolic communion, such bishops cannot assume any office."—*De Ecclesia,* n. 24.

[56] Beste, p. 852.

[57] *CIC.*, can. 1557, § 1; *Soll. Nostr.*, can. 15.

[58] *Loc. cit.*

[59] *CIC.*, can. 1557, § 2; *Soll. Nostr.*, can. 16, §§ 1, 2.

as call for a necessary court based either on theft, benefices, administration, inheritance or pious trusts,[60] the normal court for the settlement of a legal dispute is the court within whose territory the defendant lives.[61]

It follows that, insofar as the Church does declare the meaning of its own law, and has established legal procedures for the vindication of the rights of parties, the Church exhibits in its judicial department the characteristics of a juridically perfect society.

Article 3. The Church Has Coercive Power

The juridically perfect society must have the ability to demand obedience of its members through compulsion to insure that they yield to enacted laws and the same type of society must have the ability to see that these laws are obeyed under threat of penalty. The demand of conformity to the legal system of any society and the ability to punish its members is called the coercive power.[62]

When the judicial power of the Church was earlier treated a quotation was cited from Saint Matthew's Gospel wherein Our Lord stated that if a man did not heed the decision of the Church, he was to be regarded as a heathen.[63] From the words of Christ it is clear that He not only gave the Church the ability to judge the erring members but the power as well to punish such members when they refused to recede from their evil-doing. Punishment in the Church is ultimately not vindictive but remedial. The purpose of the Church in all its actions is to bring men to the fullness of Christ. If a person chooses not to heed the entreaties to emendation, then spiritual sanctions are employed with the hope that the member will realize his spiritual plight. This is the meaning of the following words of Saint Paul:

> . . . to deliver such a one over to Satan for the destruction of the flesh, that his spirit may be saved in the day of Our Lord Jesus Christ.[64]

---

[60] *CIC.*, can. 1560; *Soll. Nostr.*, can. 23.

[61] *CIC.*, can. 1559, § 3; *Soll. Nostr.*, can. 23.

[62] Cappello, p. 58.

[63] Matthew, 18: 18; *supra*, p. 30.

[64] I Corinthians, 5: 5.

The Church at present employs sanctions following the words and spirit of Saint Paul to bring the member back to sound Christian practice. The Code of Canon Law states that the Church

> . . . has the innate and proper right, independent of all human authority, to punish its guilty subjects with both spiritual and temporal penalties.[65]

This coercive power resides in the Church so that strengthened by the risen Lord

> . it might, in patience and in love, overcome its sorrows and its challenges, both within itself and from without, and that it might reveal to the world, faithfully though darkly, the mystery of its Lord until, in the end, it will be manifested in full light.[66]

From the investigation of the triple powers found resident in the Church, namely the proper legislative, judicial and coercive powers, it is evident that the Church of Christ manifests to the world the principal characteristics of every juridically perfect society.

SECTION 6. THE CHURCH IS A LEGAL PERSONALITY

The foregoing discussion on the visible structure of the Church demonstrated the Church to be a juridically perfect society. Moreover, since the Church has been commissioned to impart divine truth to all mankind

> . . . it is evident that the Church must have temporal possessions for the fulfillment of its mission. The exercise of external worship, the support of its ministers, as well as the care of orphans, of the sick and the aged, the education of youth, all involve the need of temporal possessions.[67]

---

[65] *CIC.*, can. 2214, § 1.

[66] *De Ecclesia,* n. 8.

[67] McGough, *The Laws of the State of Mississippi Affecting Church Property,* Catholic University of America Canon Law Studies, n. 417 (Washington, D. C.: The Catholic University of America Press, 1962), p. 47 (hereafter cited McGough).

The Church then must of necessity have the right to own property in its own name and behalf. In other words, the Church as such must share in the concept of moral personality. The right of ownership can only be attributed to persons, be they moral or physical. The Code of Canon Law explicitly states that the Catholic Church and the Apostolic See have the full stature of moral persons from the direct will of God.[68]

It must be noted that the universal law does not declare that the Catholic Church and the Apostolic See are in fact moral personalities. Rather, the term employed is *ratio.* The word *ratio* points in the context of canon 100 to character or nature. A moral personality is created by the public authority. A corporation, for example, is created by the public authority of the state. Inferior moral personalities exist in the Church by its own direct action.[69] Since the Church is a juridically perfect society, it has an inherent right to exist. It would be repugnant to conceive of any entity as capable of creating itself. Inasmuch as a moral personality postulates a public authority for its creation, it follows that the Church is not a moral personality in the strict sense of the term.[70] The Catholic Church and the Apostolic See have simply the nature of a moral personality, and this indeed by divine will.

There is a discussion in canonical writings with regard to the precise juridic nature of the Holy See. Some writers personify both the Church and the Holy See, stating that there is a real distinction between the two. However, the distinction is categorized as an inadequate one insofar as one is part of the other.[71] Other canonists hold that each is the possessor of a juridic personality. By divine foundation, the Holy See, i.e., the very office of the Roman episcopacy is properly a moral personality.[72] A third group would regard the Primacy of the Pope as a corporation

[68] *CIC.*, can. 100, § 1; *Cler. Sanc.*, can. 28.

[69] *CIC.*, can. 99; *Cler. Sanc.*, can. 27.

[70] *CIC.*, can. 100, § 1; *Cler. Sanc.*, can. 28.

[71] Rodriquez, *The Law of the State of New Mexico Affecting Church Property,* The Catholic University of America Canon Law Studies, n. 406 (Washington, D. C.: The Catholic University of America Press, 1959), p. 111.

[72] Abbo-Hannan, *The Sacred Canons* (2 vols., revised ed., St. Louis, Mo.: B. Herder Book Co., 1957), I, 145; Conte a Coronata, *Institutiones,* I, 159.

sole.[73] Whatever opinion is espoused it must be noted that the meaning of the Apostolic See does not in such a manner include all the Roman Congregations, Tribunals and Offices which are normally included in the term.[74]

SECTION 7 INFERIOR ECCLESIASTICAL MORAL PERSONALITIES

Article 1. Existence

The Church, entrusted with the work of bringing the Gospel to the entire world,[75] accomplishes this task as a juridically perfect society. It has the independent right and obligation of establishing subordinate moral personalities to act as its effective instruments.[76] These moral persons, unlike physical persons, are creatures of the Church. They receive existence through ecclesiastical constitution and recognition.[77] Juridical personalities are received into Canon Law under various names. They are known as *personae iuridicae,*[78] *entia iuridica,*[79] and as *personae morales.*[80] The Code of Canon Law does not give a definition of the juristic personality. This omission apparently was not an oversight, but rather it reflects a legal precaution favoring the limitations of definitions as such. The Code seems in this matter to embrace the Roman wariness of definitions.

Lawyers commenting on the meaning of moral personality have not been lacking in the attempt to give a definition to the moral personality. Conte a Coronata (1889-1961) declared that a moral personality is an entity apart from a physical person capable of

---

[73] Augustine, *A Commentary on the New Code of Canon Law* (8 vols., Vol. VI, 2, ed., St. Louis, Mo.: B. Herder Book Co., 1923), II, 7.

[74] *CIC.*, can. 7; *Postquam*, can. 302; Blat, *Commentarium Textus Codicis Iuris Canonici* (5 vols. in 7, Vol. II, 2. ed., 1921; Romae: Ex Typographia Pontificia in Institutio Pii IX, 1921), II, 36; *contra:* Abbo-Hannan, I, 145.

[75] Matthew, 28: 19-20.

[76] *CIC.*, can. 100, § 1: " inferiores personae morales"; *Cler. Sanc.*, can. 28, § 1.

[77] *CIC.*, can. 99; *Cler. Sanc.*, can. 27.

[78] *CIC.*, can. 687; *Cler. Sanc.*, can. 534.

[79] *CIC.*, can. 1409.

[80] *CIC.*, can. 99; *Cler. Sanc.*, can. 27.

rights and obligations.[81] Blat (1870-1943) considered this institute as a subject capable of possessing and exercising rights in the Church under the sacred canons.[82] These moral personalities have for their aim the spiritual or the temporal needs of the Church, since every goal of the Church is directed toward a religious or charitable end.[83]

Inferior moral personalities are completely dependent on the Church for their existence and continuation.

Article 2. Classification

Moral personalities in the Church are classified either as collegiate or non-collegiate.[84] At least three physical persons are required for the establishment of a collegiate moral personality. The personality perdures in its rights and obligations as long as a single member survives. The rights are then vested in that member. A religious community is an excellent example of a collegiate moral personality. The community has its proper personality apart from its physical members. Consequently, the rights of the community are not those of the members, nor are the debts incurred by the community enforceable against its members.[85]

The non-collegiate moral personality is not composed of physical members. Such personalities are either ecclesiastical offices and benefices, or endowments of goods destined for some public or charitable purpose, such as divine worship or the care of the poor.[86]

Article 3. Establishment and Rights

Inferior moral personalities in the Church are established in two ways. They are either created by the law (*sive ex ipso iuris praescripto*),[87] or by special decree.[88] Among the moral per-

[81] *Institutiones,* I, n. 135.

[82] *Commentarium,* II, n. 29.

[83] *CIC.,* can. 100, § 1: ". . ad finem religiosum vel caritativum."

[84] *CIC.,* can. 99; *Cler. Sanc.,* can. 27.

[85] Wernz-Vidal, *Ius Canonicum ad Normam Codicis Exactum* (7 vols. in 8, Vol. II, 3. ed., Romae: Apud Aedes Universitatis Gregorianae, 1943), 26 (hereafter cited Wernz-Vidal).

[86] Wernz-Vidal, II, n. 28.

[87] *CIC.,* can. 99; *Cler. Sanc.,* can. 27.

[88] *CIC.,* can. 100, § 1; *Cler. Sanc.,* can. 28, § 1.

sonalities created by the very provisions of the law itself, either expressly or equivalently, are the College of Cardinals,[89] the diocesan Curia,[90] and the Roman Curia.[91]

Moral personalities founded by means of a formal decree can be called corporations *ab homine* in opposition to those which are created and erected by the law. The latter may be termed corporations *a iure.*[92]

The efficient cause of moral personalities in the Church is either the Holy See or some intermediate superior with jurisdiction in the external life of the Church.[93] The formal decree consists in the explicit or implicit statement of the nature of the personality and in the concession of the personality. The erection need not be in writing but good order would seem to require that the decree should be committed to writing for permanency.[94] The Holy See is the only authority empowered to establish moral personalities of pontifical status. The following are among the moral personalities needing the papal authority: ecclesiastical provinces,[95] abbacies and prelacies *nullius,*[96] and vicariates and prefectures apostolic,[97] cathedral and collegiate chapters,[98] consistorial benefices,[99] as well as Catholic Universities and Catholic faculties.[100] The residential bishop may lawfully erect the following moral personalities: parishes,[101] hospitals and orphanages,[102] and seminaries.[103]

---

[89] *CIC.,* cans. 231, 241; *Cler. Sanc.,* cans. 176, 187.

[90] *CIC.,* can. 363; *Cler. Sanc.,* can. 429.

[91] *CIC.,* can. 242; *Cler. Sanc.,* can. 188.

[92] Beste, pp. 151-152.

[93] Michiels, *Principia Generalia de Personis in Ecclesia* (2 ed., Parisiis-Tornaci-Romae: Desclée, 1955), pp. 403-404 (hereafter cited Michiels).

[94] Regatillo, *Institutiones Iuris Canonici* (2 vols., 6 ed., Santander, Spain: Editorial Sal Terrae, 1961), I, 164 (hereafter cited Regatillo).

[95] *CIC.,* can. 248, § 2; *Cler. Sanc.,* can. 194.

[96] *CIC.,* can. 320, § 1; *Cler. Sanc.,* can. 363, §§ 1, 2.

[97] *CIC.,* can. 294, § 1.

[98] *CIC.,* can. 392; *Cler. Sanc.,* can. 465.

[99] *CIC.,* can. 1414, § 1; *Postquam,* can. 308, § 1, n. 1.

[100] *CIC.,* can. 1376, § 1.

[101] *CIC.,* can. 1414, § 2; *Cler. Sanc.,* can. 160, § 1.

[102] *CIC.,* can. 1489, § 1.

[103] *CIC.,* can. 1354.

Michiels (1890-1965) noted that the twofold manner of obtaining moral personality in the Church, i.e., from the law and from formal erection, should not be understood in a conjunctive sense. Either a personality is created by the law or through the intervention of the proper ecclesiastical authority, given in the manner of a formal decree. The mode of the acquisition of moral personality is differentiated on the basis of the personality's nature and finality. The law itself brings into existence persons either absolutely or relatively necessary for the social-public life of the Church. Conversely, moral personalities created by the special decree of a competent ecclesiastical superior are indeed not essential to the Church in the pursuit of the Church's ultimate end, but rather simply prove useful for the Church.[104]

The juridic capacity of moral personalities in ecclesiastical law is on par with the physical members of the Church. Moral personalities can acquire and possess. All the rights of physical persons may be employed by moral persons, with the exception of those rights which from the nature of the matter or from the positive provisions of law are proper to physical persons alone, as for example the right to marry.[105]

The acquired rights and possessions of moral personalities are protected by the universal law of the Church by attributing the status of minors to such personalities.[106] The predication of minority for the benefit of moral personalities follows the pattern established by Roman Law. The reason for this categorizing of moral personalities stems from the frailty of men. Just as a minor can easily suffer loss at the hands of his guardian, so, too, a moral personality acting through a human administrator can experience damage. For its protection in such a contingency, the moral personality needs the protection of the universal law in defence of its rights.[107] Moral personalities are thus represented in court by their rectors or administrators[108] similarly as physical minors

---

[104] Michiels, pp. 398-399.

[105] Michiels, p. 456.

[106] *CIC.*, can. 100, § 3; *Cler. Sanc.*, can. 28, § 3.

[107] McGough, p. 55.

[108] *CIC.*, can. 1649; *Soll. Nostr.*, can. 163, § 1.

are represented by their parents or guardians.[109] As a consequence of this juridic status, a moral person like a minor can enter a suit for a return to property (*restitutio in integrum*).[110]

It is a fundamental principle of ecclesiastical legislation that the Catholic Church and the Holy See have an inherent, unrestricted right to acquire, own and administer temporal property to accomplish the ends of their foundation, and that they hold such property independently of any civil authority.[111] Inferior moral personalities established by the universal law or by competent ecclesiastical authorities have the right to own and acquire temporalities.[112] However, since the inferior moral personalities owe existence to the lawful authority of the Church, they are subject to the norms of that authority. So, for example, the alienation of property belonging to an inferior moral personality must conform to the prescriptions of the law or the transaction is invalid.[113]

Article 4. Duration

The ecclesiastical moral personality's life is normally perpetual;[114] but, the personality may be suppressed by legitimate, public, ecclesiastical authority, or it may cease automatically when it has not evidenced any sign of life or activity for a period of one hundred years.[115] The only competent authority to suppress a moral personality is he who gave it existence, his successor in office, or a superior in jurisdiction to the foregoing.[116] There are exceptions to this general rule. The bishop is competent to erect hospitals and orphanages,[117] for instance, but he may not suppress them. The Apostolic See alone is competent to suppress these institutions.[118]

---

[109] *CIC.*, can. 1647; *Soll. Nostr.*, can. 163, § 1.
[110] *CIC.*, can. 1687, § 2; *Soll. Nostr.*, can. 432, § 1.
[111] *CIC.*, can. 1495, § 1; *Postquam*, can. 232, § 1.
[112] *CIC.*, can. 1495, § 2; *Postquam*, can. 232, § 2.
[113] *CIC.*, can. 1530, § 1, nn. 1-3; *Postquam*, can. 279, § 1, nn. 1-3.
[114] *CIC.*, can. 102, § 1; *Cler. Sanc.*, can. 30, § 1.
[115] *Loc. cit.*
[116] Abbo-Hannan, I, 149.
[117] *CIC.*, can. 1489, § 1.
[118] *CIC.*, can. 1494.

The legal extinction of an ecclesiastical moral person transpires when the institute has reflected no life or activity for one hundred years. This rule is in force regarding both collegiate and non-collegiate personalities. In the former case, the demise of the moral personality takes place *de iure* with the death or resignation of every member of the group and without any concurrent replacement of the institute's members. If there be but one surviving member, all the rights and powers of the moral personality are centered in the one survivor.[119] The collegiate moral personality may also expire upon the voluntary act of the group dissolving itself.

The non-collegiate personality's demise is verified *de iure* when the substratum of goods is entirely destroyed or irrevocably removed from its possession. Michiels evidences such a course of events when a church is totally destroyed or has become so deteriorated that divine services are impossible there.[120]

There is an equivalent extinction of a moral personality when the juridic personality severs its union with the Church, either through heresy or schism. Since there is an obstacle to the unity with the visible bond of union in the Church[121] the existence, rights and prerogatives granted by the Church automatically cease.[122]

The property owned by moral personalities will, upon the cessation of their existence, belong to the moral personality immediately superior to the defunct personality, granted the proper fulfillment of the will and intentions of the legally vested rights, and also of special laws governing the extinct moral personality.[123]

---

[119] *CIC.*, can. 102, § 2; *Cler. Sanc.*, can. 30, § 2.

[120] Michiels, p. 542.

[121] *CIC.*, can. 87; *Cler. Sanc.*, can. 16.

[122] Vromant, *De Bonis Temporalibus* (3. ed., Bruges-Paris: Desclée de Brouwer, 1953), p. 23.

[123] *CIC.*, can. 1501; *Postquam*, can. 238.

CHAPTER III

The Roman Catholic Church Under the Constitution of the United States of America

SECTION 1. THE ESTABLISHMENT CLAUSE

The phraseology of the "establishment" clause of the First Amendment together with the judicial interpretations of this Amendment circumscribe the civil position of the Roman Catholic Church in the United States of America. The Constitution did not reject religion as a proper concern of the American people. Rather than adopting such a policy of eighteenth century European indifferentism, the constitutional framers sought to guarantee the freedom of each man's conscience by severely limiting legislative competence in this crucial area of civil liberty.[1] The *Bloom v. Richards* decision clearly demonstrated that the Constitution sought the security of religious liberty. The decision in part stated:

> . . . we sometimes hear it said that all religions are tolerated in Ohio, but the expression is not strictly accurate; much less is it to say, that one religion is part of our law, and all others only tolerated. It is not by mere tolerance that every individual here is protected in his belief or disbelief. He reposes not upon the leniency of government, or the liberality of any class or sect of men, but upon his natural, indefeasible rights of conscience, which, in the language of the Constitution, are beyond the control of Church and State, nor has our government been vested with authority to enforce any religious observance, simply because it is religious.[2]

---

[1] Kauper, *Religion and the Constitution* (Kingsport, Tenn.: Louisiana University Press, 1964), p. 46: ". . . a principal historical purpose underlying the establishment clause was to state a jurisdictional limitation on Congress by denying it power to interfere with state religious establishments. It made clear that this was not a subject within the competence of the federal government."

[2] *Bloom v. Richards,* 2 Ohio 387 (1853).

In the beginning of this country's history only Congress was impeded from enacting laws concerning religion. State legislators were still in theory able to pass religious centered legislation. The passage of the Fourteenth Amendment and its gradual application to the First Amendment gave rise to a series of decisions imposing upon the various States identical restrictions as imposed on Congress. *The Cantwell v. Connecticut* trial[3] brought the first explicit application of the First Amendment limitation to the States.

Three general theories have been enunciated by the Supreme Court detailing the legal construction of the "establishment" clause of the First Amendment. At first, the Supreme Court saw an absolute separation of church and state as the proper construction of the First Amendment. A theory of modified accommodation was the next formulation introduced by the Court. The third and current understanding of the First Amendment is that of neutrality. It must not be imagined that each theory is a repudiation of earlier constructions. Rather, each opinion gave birth to the succeeding view.

Article 1. The Absolute Theory

The initial declaration of the absolute view of the First Amendment was given by the Supreme Court in 1878 in the case of *Reynolds v. United States.*[4] The *Reynolds* decision incorporated for the first time the famous phrase "wall of separation." The words were taken from a letter of Thomas Jefferson (1743-1826). The Supreme Court using Jefferson's words placed an absolute construction on the First Amendment.

The *Reynolds* case was not an establishment case as such. The case turned on the right of a citizen to act in conformity with his religious principles. Congress had passed laws making bigamy within federal territories a criminal offense. The appellant attempted to enter a second marriage in accordance with his religious principles. He

> . proved that at the time of his alleged second marriage, he was, and for many years before had been, a

[3] *Cantwell v. Connecticut,* 310 U.S. 296, 60 S. Ct. 980, 84 L. Ed. 1213.

[4] *Reynolds v. United States,* 98 U.S. 145, 25 L. Ed. 244 (1878).

> member of the Church of Jesus Christ of Latter Day Saints, commonly called the Mormon Church, and a believer in its doctrine; that it was an accepted doctrine of that Church that it was the duty of male members of said Church, circumstances permitting, to practice polygamy . . . that the failing or refusing to practice polygamy by such members of said Church, when circumstances would admit, would be punished, and that the penalty for such failure and refusal would be damnation in the world to come.[5]

The Supreme Court held that, although Congress did not have the right to legislate religious beliefs, nevertheless, such beliefs did not constitute a legal defense justifying an overt criminal act in contravention of a duly enacted statute.

> Here the accused knew he had been once married and that his first wife was living. He also knew that his second marriage was forbidden by law. When, therefore, he married the second time, he is presumed to have intended to break the law. And the breaking of the law is the crime. . . . It matters not that his belief was a part of his professed religion; it was still belief, and belief only.[6]

The Court came to its decision after considering the meaning of religion, the meaning of the First Amendment, and the right of Congress to enact laws in conformity with the public needs. The Court recognized that religion was not defined by the Constitution. It also elected not to offer a definition. The Court rather chose to embrace the definition of religion given by Thomas Jefferson. Jefferson regarded religion as a personal opinion regarding the relationship of a man with his Creator.[7] The Court held that this relationship meaning underlay the "establishment" clause of the First Amendment. The clause sprung, said the Court, from the widespread disestablishment of colonial churches, and, in par-

---

[5] *Loc. cit.*

[6] *Loc. cit.*

[7] Jefferson was invited to address a committee of the Danbury Baptist Association. In his letter to the group he took the occasion to say "Believing with you that religion is a matter which lies solely between man and his God: that he owes account to none other for his faith or worship. . "

ticular, the Amendment reflected the disestablishment of the church in the Virginia colony.

With this as its historical background, the Court accepted the Jeffersonian concept that the framers of the Constitution had as their prime purpose the desire to erect a strict "wall of separation between the Church and the State."[8] The Court then went on to declare:

> Coming as this does from an acknowledged leader of the advocates of the measure, it may be accepted almost as an authoritative declaration of the scope and effect of the amendment thus secured. Congress was deprived of all legislative power over mere opinion, but was left free to reach actions which were violative of social duties or subversive of good order.[9]

The Court in embracing the Jeffersonian understanding of establishment thus embraced the first of the three meanings of the First Amendment's "establishment" clause. The Court viewed the Church and State as separated by an insurmountable wall. But, it cannot be too strongly emphasized that the American judicial construction of the separation of Church and State bore no resemblance to the Church and State separation of European Jacobinism.[10]

The Court also affirmed that although religious views are outside the scope of legislative competence, nevertheless, practices touching on public purposes did constitute a proper legislative purpose. Acts contravening these duly passed laws could not be excused on the grounds of religious beliefs. Reynolds' conviction was sustained, not because of his religious beliefs, but because his actions violated a public purpose statute. The Court stated that polygamy ". . . has always been odious among northern and western nations of Europe."[11] The legislatures had a vital interest in marriage according to the Court.

> Upon it [marriage] society may be said to be built, and out of its fruits spring social relations and social obliga-

---

[8] *Reynolds v. United States,* 98 U.S. 145, 25 L. Ed. 244.

[9] *Loc. cit.*

[10] *Infra,* p. 61.

[11] *Reynolds v. United States,* 98 U.S. 145, 25 L. Ed. 244.

> tions and duties, with which government is necessarily required to deal. . . . In our opinion, the statute immediately under consideration is within the legislative power of Congress. It is constitutional and valid as prescribing a rule of action for all those residing in the Territories, and in places over which the United States have exclusive control. This being so, the only question which remains, is, whether those who make polygamy a part of their religion are exempted from the operation of this statute. . . Laws are made for the government of actions, and while they cannot interfere with mere opinions, they may with practice. . . Can a man excuse his practices to the contrary because of his religious belief? To permit this would be to make the professed doctrines of religious belief superior to the law of the land, and in effect to permit every citizen to become a law unto himself.[12]

The decision of the *Reynolds* case was elaborated upon and "establishment" was detailed in the case of *Everson v. Board of Education.*[13] The case was a result of payments made by the township of Ewing, New Jersey, to compensate parents for the costs of transporting children to private non-profit schools. The payments were made pursuant to a state statute and a resolution adopted by Ewing's school board. The New Jersey statute stated:

> Whenever in any school district there are children living remote from any school house, the board of education of the district may make rules and contracts for the transportation of children to and from school other than a public school, except such school as is operated for a profit in whole or part. When any school district provides any transportation for public school children to and from school, transportation from any point in such established school route to any other point in such established school route shall be supplied to school children residing in such school district in going to and from school other than a public school, except such school as is operated for profit in whole or in part. Nothing in this section shall be construed as to prohibit a board of education from making contracts for the transportation of children

[12] *Loc. cit.*

[13] *Everson v. Board of Education,* 330 U.S. 1, 67 S. Ct. 504, 91 L. Ed. 711 (1947).

> to a school in an adjoining district when such children are transferred to the district by order of the county superintendent of schools, or when any children shall attend school in a district other than in which they shall reside by virtue of an agreement made by the respective boards of education.[14]

A taxpayer brought suit contending the statute was an establishment of religion. The Supreme Court decision was read by Mr. Justice Black (1886-). The opinion recognized that the First Amendment placed a legislative inhibition basically on the Congress of the United States in its original form. However, the Court enlarged the application of the Amendment in conformity to the due process clause of the Fourteenth Amendment.

> The broad meaning given the Amendment by . earlier cases has been accepted by this Court in its decisions concerning an individual's religious freedom rendered since the Fourteenth Amendment was interpreted to make the prohibitions of the First applicable to state action abridging religious freedom. There is every reason to give the same application and broad interpretation to the "establishment of religion" clause.[15]

The Court then gave its understanding of the "establishment" clause.

> The "establishment of religion" clause of the First Amendment means at least this: Neither a state nor the Federal Government can set up a church. Neither can pass laws which aid one religion, aid all religions, or prefer one religion over another. Neither can force nor influence a person to go to, or to remain away from, church against his will, or force him to profess a belief or disbelief in any religion. No person can be punished for entertaining or professing religious beliefs or disbeliefs, for church attendance or non-attendance. No tax in any amount, large or small, can be levied to support any religious activities or institutions, whatever they may

---

[14] *Loc. cit.*

[15] *Loc. cit.*

> be called, or whatever form they may adopt to teach or practice religion. Neither a state nor the Federal Government can, openly or secretly, participate in the affairs of any religious organization or groups and vice versa. In the words of Jefferson, the clause against the establishment of religion by law was intended to erect "a wall of separation between church and state."[16]

The opinion of the Court prohibited not only a preference of one religion over others but the equal support of all religions. The position mirrored Jefferson's belief that religion is so vital a concern that no group of legislators may dare to intrude into the area of man's relationship with his Maker. The prohibition of aid to all religions as such is the distinctive element of the Everson decision. The opinion effectively precludes the establishment of one religion or multiple establishments of the variety of religions within the United States.[17]

Having given its meaning of the "establishment" clause, the Court juxtaposed the facts of the New Jersey allotment to the *Everson* doctrine. The Court saw no violation of the First Amendment in New Jersey's statute or Ewing's practices. The State of New Jersey could constitutionally sustain the expenses incurred by the parents in transporting their children to the private non-profit schools. The purpose the Court observed was not an establishment of religion but a public purpose statute designed to protect the school children from the hazards of traffic.

> We must consider the New Jersey statute in accordance with the foregoing limitations imposed by the First Amendment. But we must not strike that state statute down if it is within the State's constitutional power even though it approaches the verge of that power. New Jersey cannot consistently with the "establishment of religion" clause of the First Amendment contribute tax raised funds to the support of an institution which teaches the tenets and faith of any church. On the other hand, other language of the amendment commands that New Jersey cannot hamper its children in the free exercise of their

---

[16] *Loc. cit.*

[17] Kauper, *Religion and the Constitution,* p. 61.

> own religion. . . . Measured by these standards, we cannot say that the First Amendment prohibits New Jersey from spending tax-raised funds to pay the bus fares of parochial school pupils as a part of a general program under which it pays the fares of pupils attending public and other schools. . . . This Court has said that parents may . . . in the discharge of their duty under state compulsory education laws, send their children to a religious rather than a public school if the school meets the secular educational requirements which the state has the power to impose. It appears that these parochial schools meet New Jersey's requirements. The State contributes no money to the schools. It does not support them. Its legislation, as applied, does no more than provide a general program to help parents get their children, regardless of their religion, safely and expeditiously to and from accredited school.[18]

The strict wall enunciated by *Reynolds*[19] and detailed by *Everson*[20] was used one year later in the case of *McCollum v. Board of Education*.[21] The City of Champaign, Illinois, through its Board of Education, permitted the inter-faith Champaign Council on Religious Education to conduct religion classes in the public school classrooms during school hours. Parents who desired their children to participate in the instructions filled out a card requesting that their children be allowed to attend the religion classes. The classes were under the supervision of teachers the Council secured for the religious program. The instructors were supplied gratis to the school system. The teachers, however, had to secure the approval of the superintendent of schools. Children were placed into groups according to their faith and were taught in the classrooms of the public school. Students whose parents did not desire their children's participation in the religious program were required to leave their classrooms, go to another part of the school, and there to receive instruction in secular topics. Students actively partic-

---

[18] *Everson v. Board of Education*, 330 U.S. 1, 67 S. Ct. 504, 91 L. Ed. 711.

[19] *Reynolds v. United States*, 98 U.S. 145, 25 L. Ed. 244.

[20] *Everson v. Board of Education*, 330 U.S. 1, 67 S. Ct. 504, 91 L. Ed. 711.

[21] *McCollum v. Board of Education*, 333 U.S. 203, 68 S. Ct. 461, 92 L. Ed. 649 (1948).

ipating in the religious instructions were compelled to attend the instructions under penalty of truancy.

Mrs. Vashiti McCollum, mother of one of the children not attending the religion classes, brought suit to challenge the constitutional validity of the program. She was upheld. The Supreme Court's decision given by Mr. Justice Black stated:

> The foregoing facts, without reference to others that appear in the record, show the use of tax-supported property for religious instruction and the close cooperation between school authorities and the religious council in promoting education. The operation of the State's compulsory education system thus assists and is integrated with the program of religious instruction carried on by separate religious sects. Pupils compelled by law to go to school for secular education are released in part from their legal duty upon the condition that they attend the religious classes. This is beyond all question a utilization of the tax-established and tax-supported public school system to aid religious groups to spread their faith. And it falls squarely under the ban of the First Amendment (made applicable to the States by the Fourteenth) as we interpreted in *Everson v. Board of Education*. . . To hold that a State cannot consistently with the First and Fourteenth Amendments utilize its public school system to aid one or all religions or sects in the dissemination of their doctrines and ideals does not, as counsel urge, manifest a government hostility to religion or religious teachings. A manifestation of such hostility would be at war with our national tradition as embodied in the First Amendment's guarantee of the free exercise of religion. For the First Amendment rests upon the premise that both religion and government can best work to achieve their lofty aims if each is left free from the other within its respective sphere. Or, as we said in the *Everson* case, the First Amendment has erected a wall between Church and State which must be kept high and impregnable.[22]

The Everson doctrine was restated in two later cases which received a degree of notoriety. In 1961 the Supreme Court declared a section of the Maryland Constitution unconstitutional in *Torcaso*

[22] *Loc. cit.*

v. Watkins.[23] Article 37 of the Declaration of Rights of Maryland's Constitution stated:

> . . . [N]o religious test ought ever to be required as a qualification for any office of profit or trust in this State, other than a declaration of belief in the existence of God. . . .[24]

The appellant was denied his appointed commission as a notary public upon his refusal to declare a belief in God. He sought Court relief contending that the state's requirement violated the First and Fourteenth Amendments. The Supreme Court ruled in Mr. Torcaso's favor. Mr. Justice Black read the majority opinion. He reaffirmed the absolute separation theory enunciated by himself in the *Everson* Judgment.

> . . . We repeat and again affirm that neither a State nor the Federal Government can constitutionally force a person "to profess a belief or disbelief in any religion." Neither can constitutionally pass laws or impose requirements which aid all religions as against non-believers, and neither can aid those religious based on a belief in the existence of God as against those religions founded on different beliefs. . . . This Maryland religious test for public office unconstitutionally invades the appellant's freedom of belief and religion and therefore cannot be enforced against him.[25]

In 1962 the "wall of separation" was again supported in the case of *Engel v. Vitale.*[26] The New York State Board of Regents had formulated a non-sectarian prayer. The Board recommended the prayer's daily recitation in all the public schools. The prayer read:

> Almighty God, we acknowledge our dependence on Thee, and we beg Thy blessing upon us, our parents, our teachers, and our country.[27]

---

[23] *Torcaso v. Watkins,* 367 U.S. 488, 81 S. Ct. 1680, 6 L. Ed. 2d. 982 (1961).

[24] *Loc. cit.*

[25] *Loc. cit.*

[26] *Engel v. Vitale,* 370 U.S. 421, 82 S. Ct. 1261, 8 L. Ed. 2d. 601 (1962).

[27] *Loc. cit.*

Parents of ten children brought action to enjoin the continuation of the prayer contending that such a recitation was a violation of the "establishment" clause of the First Amendment. They further argued that the state's action by virtue of the Fourteenth Amendment was itself unconstitutional. Mr. Justice Black again delivered the Court's majority opinion. He ruled that the prayer was unconstitutional in as much as the State's action was inconsistent with the "establishment" clause of the First Amendment.

> We think that by using its public school system to encourage recitation of the Regents' prayer, the State of New York's program of daily classroom invocation of God's blessings as prescribed in the Regents' prayer is a religious activity. It is a solemn avowal of divine faith and supplication for the blessings of the Almighty. The nature of such a prayer has always been religious; none of the respondents has denied this. . . . The petitioners contend among other things that the state law requiring or permitting a use of the Regents' prayer must be struck down as a violation of the Establishment Clause because that prayer was composed by government officials as a part of a government program to further religious beliefs. For this reason, petitioners argue, the State's use of the Regents' prayer in its public school system breaches the constitutional wall of separation between Church and State. We agree with that contention, since we think that the constitutional prohibition against laws respecting an establishment of religion must at least mean that in this country it is no part of the business of government to compose official prayers for any group of the American people to recite as part of a religious program carried on by the government.[28]

The foregoing cases, based on the *Reynolds*[29] acceptation of Jefferson's understanding of the First Amendment, rest on the conjunctive consideration of the citizen's right to freely exercise his religion. In order to secure the maximum exercise of this right, the individual must be free from all legislative encumbrances. Therefore, the federal and state government are required to

---

[28] *Loc. cit.*

[29] *Reynolds v. United States,* 98 U.S. 145, 25 L. Ed. 244.

offer no aid or support indicating governmental preference or influence.[30]

It must be noted that the "wall of separation" theory in church and state relations did not preclude all governmental cooperation with religion. If a governmental program, as in the case of *Everson*, i.e., bus transportation, did benefit indirectly a religious practice or denomination, the program would not be unconstitutional simply for this reason. Provided there was a valid public purpose, a measure aiding a religion indirectly could be sustained.

Article 2. The Accommodation Theory

The "wall of separation" doctrine was mitigated somewhat as it gave rise to the accommodation theory reflecting the nature of the "establishment clause." The Supreme Court announced this view of the First Amendment in the case of *Zorach v. Clauson.*[31] The *Zorach* litigation grew out of the released time legislation in the State of New York. New York passed provisions for a voluntary program of religious instructions to be carried out during school hours, but away from public school buildings. Parents, wishing their children to participate in such instructions, presented a written request at the opening of the school year. The schools were thereby authorized to release the children for the last hour or the last class period on the day of religious instructions. The children were brought to religion centers at the parents' expense. The New York program differed from the circumstances of the *McCollum* case[32] in that the children were removed from public school grounds. Nor was there any psychological pressure brought to bear on the children who did not participate in the religious instructions. Non-participating children remained in school and in their classrooms if they did not seek the religious instructions available for them. Hence, there was no direct or indirect compulsion on children to participate or to remain aloof from the program.

---

[30] Kauper, *Religion and the Law*, p. 59.

[31] *Zorach v. Clauson,* 343 U.S. 306, 72 S. Ct. 679, 96 L. Ed. 954 (1952).

[32] *McCollum v. Board of Education,* 333 U.S. 203, 68 S. Ct. 461, 92 L. Ed. 649.

The Supreme Court viewed the two cases as decidedly distinct. In stating the heart of the question, Mr. Justice Douglas (1898-) wrote in the majority opinion:

> . . . our problem reduces itself to whether New York by this system has either prohibited the "free exercise" of religion or has made a law "respecting an establishment of religion" within the meaning of the First Amendment.[33]

Mr. Justice Douglas saw no evidence indicating that the case presented any issues infringing upon the "free exercise" clause for the "establishment" clause. The decision pointed out that the wall of separation envisioned by the *Everson*[34] and *McCollum*[35] decisions cannot be taken in an absolute sense in each and every encounter of the state and the various churches composing the Union. While maintaining the theory of the separation of Church and State as "complete and unequivocal,"[36] Mr. Justice Douglas stated:

> The First Amendment, however, does not say that in every and all respects there shall be a separation of Church and State. Rather, it studiously defines the matter, the specific ways, in which there shall be no concert or union or dependency one on the other.[37]

The "moderate approach"[38] taken by Mr. Justice Douglas reflects his appreciation of the religious feelings of the American people. He observed that much had been stated regarding the separation of Church and State; but, he also pointed out that the American people are not aliens with respect to God.

> We are a religious people whose institutions presuppose a Supreme Being. We guarantee the freedom to worship as one chooses.[39]

---

33 *Zorach v. Clauson,* 343 U.S. 306, 72 S. Ct. 679, 96 L. Ed. 954.

34 *Everson v. Board of Education,* 330 U.S. 1, 67 S. Ct. 504, 91 L. Ed. 711.

35 *McCollum v. Board of Education,* 333 U.S. 203, 68 S. Ct. 461, 92 L. Ed. 649.

36 *Zorach v. Clauson,* 343 U.S. 306, 72 S. Ct. 679, 96 L. Ed. 954.

37 *Loc. cit.*

38 Kauper, *Religion and the Constitution,* p. 67.

39 *Loc. cit.*

Noting that government may not finance religious groups or give religious services, Mr. Justice Douglas remarked that the government may indeed accommodate itself to the religious needs of the people. Moreover, the contrary view which would demand that the government offer not even a modicum of its protective arm to religion would imply an open hostility. Such a course of action would be contrary to the practice of the country. Cities, according to the absolutistic logic carried to the furthest degree, would act unconstitutionally should they offer police or fire protection. Aid given by a policeman to a person crossing the street on the way to church would be a similar violation of the Constitution. No prayer could be offered in Congress. Messages of the President proclaiming Thanksgiving Day would be unconstitutional. Taking note of the *McCollum* case,[40] and stating their belief in the separation principle therein, the Court refused to go the route of some absolutists who see in the First Amendment the obligation of hostility to religion. The interpretation of hostility is not part of the American legal pattern. "We cannot read into the Bill of Rights such a philosophy of hostility to religion."[41]

Article 3. The Neutrality Theory

The meaning of the *Zorach* decision became clouded in the following decade. There seemed to be an express withdrawal from the principles of voluntary accommodation. The term "voluntary" is used because the *Zorach* decision was predicated on the *beneplacitum* of the State. The State was free to go along with some measures of accommodation, or the State could constitutionally abstain. In the case of *Engel v. Vitale*[42] the doctrine of absolutism stated in the *Everson* decision[43] once again appeared as the judicial interpretation of the Supreme Court. The pragmatic and historically accepted theory of voluntary accommodation appeared to be set aside.

---

[40] *McCollum v. Board of Education,* 333 U.S. 203, 68 S. Ct. 461, 92 L. Ed. 649.

[41] *Zorach v. Clauson,* 343 U.S. 306, 72 S. Ct. 679, 96 L. Ed. 954.

[42] *Engel v. Vitale,* 370 U.S. 421, 82 S. Ct. 1261, 8 L. Ed. 2d. 601.

[43] *Everson v. Board of Education,* 330 U.S. 1, 67 S. Ct. 504, 91 L. Ed. 711.

The *Everson* doctrine[44], restated in the *Engel* decision,[45] was altered in 1963. In the case of *School District of Abington Township v. Schempp*[46] the Supreme Court read into the First Amendment a new construction. In place of the absolute incapacity of the State to aid one, all, or to voluntarily cooperate with religion on the other hand, the Court espoused the new doctrine of neutrality. It is true that the term neutrality was used in the decision of Mr. Justice Black in *Everson v. Board of Education.*[47] However in the *Schempp* opinion, the understanding of neutrality was explained. The implications of its meaning as detailed by the Supreme Court far exceeded the no-aid neutrality of the Everson decision.[48]

The *School District of Abington Township v. Schempp*[49] decision was conjoined with another case, *Murray v. Curlett.*[50] Both cases turned on the right of public schools to have religious practices conducted during school hours. The *Schempp* case called into question the Pennsylvania statute requiring a reading without comment of ten verses from the Holy Bible. The verses were read at the opening of the school day. The law made provisions for excusing any child from this practice upon the presentation of a written request by his parent or guardian. The *Murray* case involved no statutory law. Mrs. Murray sought redress from her son's obligation of attending the daily reading from the Holy Bible and the recitation of the Lord's Prayer. These practices were in accordance with a 1905 regulation adopted by the City Board of School Commissioners of Baltimore, Maryland.

Mr. Justice Clark (1898-) gave the majority opinion of the Court in both cases, which were conjoined. He noted that the nation had indeed a close relation with religion. The belief of the

---

[44] *Loc. cit.*

[45] *Engel v. Vitale,* 370 U.S. 421, 82 S. Ct. 1261, 8 L. Ed. 2d. 601.

[46] *School District of Abington Township v. Schempp,* 374 U.S. 203, 83 S. Ct. 1560, 10 L. Ed. 2d. 844 (1963).

[47] *Everson v. Board of Education,* 330 U.S. 1, 67 S. Ct. 504, 91 L. Ed. 711.

[48] *Loc. cit.*

[49] *School District of Abington Township v. Schempp,* 374 U.S. 203, 83 S. Ct. 1560, 10 L. Ed. 2d. 844.

[50] *Loc. cit.*

founding fathers and the practices of oaths calling God's witness to the truth of statements all indicate the intermingling of the presence of God within the American framework of government. It is also equally true, Mr. Justice Clark noted, that religious freedom is indispensable in as variegated a culture as the one of the United States.

> . . . But, the First Amendment, in its final form, did not simply bar a congressional enactment *establishing a church;* it forbade all laws *respecting an establishment of religion.* Thus, this Court has given the Amendment a "broad interpretation" . . . in the light of its history and the evils it was designed forever to suppress.[51]

With this understanding, the Court struck down the practices of the State of Pennsylvania and the City of Baltimore. Their respective actions were violations of the "establishment" clause of the First Amendment. The legislatures in passing statutes must hold themselves completely neutral. Resting this decision on an unpublished opinion, the Court held that the ideal of the American people as evidenced in the First Amendment is "absolute equality before the law, of all religious opinions and sects."[52]

Since the universal judicial understanding of the First Amendment was to withdraw power to enact laws respecting an "establishment" of religion, the Court held that the proper test of all legislation should be:

> . . what are the purpose and primary effect of the enactment? If these are either the advancement or the inhibition of religion, then the enactment exceeds the scope of legislative power as circumscribed by the Constitution. This is to say that to withstand the strictures of the Establishment Clause there must be a secular purpose and a primary effect that neither advances nor inhibits religion. . . . The Free Exercise Clause, likewise considered many times here, withdraws from legislative power, state and federal, the exertion of any restraint on the free exercise of religion. Its purpose is to secure religious liberty in the individual by prohibiting any invasions thereof by civil authority. Hence it is necessary in a free exercise case for one to show the coercive effect

[51] *Loc. cit.*

[52] *Loc. cit.*

> of the enactment as it operates against him in the practice of his religion. The distinction between the two clauses in apparent a violation of the Free Exercise Clause is predicated on coercion while the Establishment Clause violation need not be so attended.[53]

The same day the Court ruled on the *Schempp* and *Murray* cases it handed down another decision which further elucidates the principles of neutrality that must control any legislation that has religious overtones. In *Sherbert v. Verner*[54] the appellant was a member of the Seventh Day Adventist Church. She was discharged by her South Carolina employer because she refused to work on Saturday, the Sabbath of her faith. She was unable to secure any other position due to her religious scruples of working on Saturday, and therefore made application for unemployment compensation. The State Commission denied her application for compensation, holding that she would not accept offered work. The ruling was sustained by South Carolina's Supreme Court. On appeal to the United States Supreme Court, Mr. Justice Brennan (1906-) in the majority opinion held that the State of South Carolina had violated the appellant's constitutional rights.

> We turn first to the question whether the disqualification for benefits imposes any burden on the free exercise of the appellant's religion. We think it is clear that it does. . . . Here not only is it apparent that appellant's declared ineligibility for benefits derives solely from the practice of her religion, but the pressure upon her to forego that practice is unmistakable. The ruling forces her to choose between following the precepts of her religion and forfeiting benefits, on the one hand and abandoning one of the precepts of her religion in order to accept work, on the other hand.[55]

This decision presents a clear picture of a state law of general operation imposing an indirect burden on religious liberty. Only a compelling state interest would secure the constitutionality of the general law, which interest was not present in this case. The

---

[53] *Loc. cit.*

[54] *Sherbert v. Verner,* 374 U.S. 398, 83 S. Ct. 1790, 10 L. Ed., 2d. 965 (1963).

[55] *Loc. cit.*

case affirms the conclusion that *religious liberty* is recognized as an independent liberty occupying a preferred place, and that the Court will admit no encroachments without a compelling and clear public necessity.[56]

Neutrality is not a pleasant doctrine to which "religious" legislators must offer lip service. Rather, just as no legislation may be passed that directly fosters religious practices, so too no legislation may be enacted that even indirectly would remove the preferred right of religious exercise without the gravest of causes. The right of the free exercise of religious beliefs holds a preferred position in the United States. Legislatures, in virtue of the *Sherbert* decision, must see to it that no action they perform would mitigate this basic liberty of the citizens. It would not be unconstitutional to pass laws that indirectly aid religion, provided there be a primary public purpose; but it would be unconstitutional to pass laws that indirectly prohibit the free exercise of religious beliefs.

In 1965 a case was returned to the local tribunals to be acted on in accordance with the *Sherbert* decision. *In Re Jenison*[57] was a case in which the Supreme Court was asked to pass on the constitutionality of a state law demanding that a citizen act as a juror when the person felt barred from so acting in view of religious principles. Just as in the *Sherbert* case, the appellant had been placed in a position either of foregoing her religious scruples or of facing legislative punishments. The Supreme Court in applying the *Sherbert* doctrine to the *Jenison* case reinforced the provisions of the theory of necessary rather than voluntary neutrality on the part of government agencies.

SECTION 2. THE RELATIONSHIP OF THE FIRST AMENDMENT AND PAPAL DOCTRINE ON CHURCH AND STATE

Article 1. Introduction

The present controlling doctrine in reference to the First Amendment meaning is found in the *Schempp* case.[58] The case

---

[56] Kauper, *Religion and the Constitution,* p. 43.

[57] *In Re Jenison,* 375 U.S. 14, 84 S. Ct. 136, 11 L. Ed. 2d. 45 (1965).

[58] *School District of Abington Township v. Schempp,* 374 U.S. 203, 83 S. Ct. 1560, 10 L. Ed. 2d. 844.

states a political, judicial doctrine. The Constitution is a political compact. It does not state a theological doctrine. The Constitution is designed to give a *modus vivendi* in a pragmatic political sphere with a view to insuring the rights of citizens of the United States.

The ultimate goal of each man is his union with Christ. This eternal destiny is not the immediate goal of the American political establishment. The Constitution was meant to be the tool of politics to secure the natural blessings of domestic tranquillity for the citizens of America. The statements of the Constitution, then, are not pronouncements of theology; rather, they evidence a profession of the public policy of the citizens in the temporal order.

> If these clauses are made articles of faith . . . there are immediately in this country 30,000,000 dissenters, the Catholic community. . . . If it be true that the First Amendment is to be given a theological interpretation and that therefore it must be "believed," made an object of religious faith, it would follow that a religious test has been thrust into the Constitution.[59]

The First Amendment had the same goal as the rest of the Constitution, the goal of peace and tranquillity within the political society. The Amendment was never a dogma of religious faith. It was a statement of political expedience coupled with a basic realization of the freedom of the citizen to worship as his conscience dictates. The Constitution was framed not by theologians but by politicians. These lawyers, farmers and craftsmen, the colonial leaders, were motivated by temporal concerns. Such a statement may appear fundamental. However, often the words of the First Amendment are used by some either as a dogmatic profession or by others as an attempt to place before the minds of men the ineffectuality of all religions. Neither views could be further from the truth.

> American separation of Church and State, unlike the Continental brand, neither implies nor effects any sac-

[59] Murray, "The Problem of Pluralism in America," *Thought,* XXIX (1954), 187-188; in 1966 there would be approximately 44,000,000 Catholic dissenters.

> ralization of politics. The First Amendment has no religious overtones whatever. . . . Its purpose is not to separate religion from society, but only from the order of law. It implies no denial of the sovereignty of God over both society and state. . . . It is not a political transcription of the religious laicism. It is a legal rule, not a piece of secular ecclesiology.[60]

The American Constitution offers no attack on the dogmatic teachings of the Catholic Church. The Constitution and the judicial interpretations recognize the two orders of man; the relationship of man with his God, and the relationship of man with his fellow citizens. Both orders are predicated on service to the Creator. Both orders call upon the guidance and grace of Almighty God.

Article 2. Pope Leo XIII (1878-1903)

Pope Leo XIII detailed the ideal relationship between a democracy and the Church. Leo placed before all men the necessity of man's acknowledgment of his God. Man, the Pontiff stated, moves in two orders simultaneously.

> The Almighty, therefore, has given charge of the human race to two powers, the ecclesiastical and the civil, the one being set over divine, and the other human things. Each in its kind is supreme, each has fixed limits within which it is contained, limits which are defined by the nature and special object of the province of each, so that there is, we may say, an orbit traced within which the action of each is brought into play by its own native right.[61]

Because man is not a dichotomy, but an integral individual, the two communities, the community of God and the community of the political order can never be absolutely separated. To separate them would be to have a difformity within the framework of creation. The ideal relationship of the two spheres, the Church and

---

[60] Murray, "Leo XIII: Separation of Church and State" *Theological Studies,* XIV (1953), 152-153.

[61] Leo XIII, *Immortale Dei, ASS,* XVIII (1885); translation: *The Church Speaks to the Modern World,* p. 162.

State being in close harmony, should inevitably lead to the establishment of the Catholic Church as the established religion.[62]

Leo XIII went on to point out that the Church . .

> does not, on that account, condemn those rulers who, for the sake of securing some great good or of hindering some great evil, allow patiently custom or usage to be a kind of sanction for every kind of religion having its place in the State.[63]

The intelligent appreciation of the Pontiff's words demands placing his statements in their proper historical context. The Pope is not issuing his statement concerning democracy against the background of the democratic form of government as experienced in the United States.

> The State for which Leo outlined the ideal relationship to the Church was a paternal state. Leo recognized that the organization or society might rightfully take different shapes to fit varying indigenous needs. But whatever legitimate shape the organization of society took, Leo presupposed that it would be paternal. The only strictly non-paternal organization of society which Leo acknowledged as distinctive was the godless and anti-Christian democracy of the Jacobins. There was, of course, no need and no possibility of a satisfactory, much less ideal, relationship between the Church and such a political organization. The possibility and implications of a responsible democratic society which was neither paternal nor Jacobin, Leo seems never to have expressly conceived, at least as far as his writings indicate.[64]

The view of Father Regan as stated above is shared by Father Murray,[65] Father Gustave Weigel (1906-1964),[66] and Doctor

---

[62] *Immortale Dei;* translation, *op. cit.*, p. 164: ". . . the State . is clearly bound to act up to the manifold and weighty duties linking it to God, by the profession of religion. . . "

[63] *Immortale Dei;* translation, *op. cit.*, p. 178.

[64] Regan, *American Pluralism and the Catholic Conscience* (New York: Macmillan Company, 1963), pp. 49-50 (hereafter cited Regan).

[65] "Leo XIII: Two Concepts of Government," *Theological Studies* XIV (1953), p. 567: The doctrines of Pope Leo ". . repose to some extent on a concept of government as paternal . . . a concept which is hypothetically and historically conditioned. . . . Leo XIII accepted the analogy, common

Raymond Schmidt.[67] These historians equate paternalism and democracy in the mind of Leo XIII.

Furthermore, as a political institution the United States is a vastly different entity from the democracies experienced by Pope Leo. The United States is a political reality flowing from the common consent of the citizens, and not from any paternalistic group within the society. Leo had not experienced the unique form of government as it existed in the United States.[68]

> It is now coming to be recognized that the Church opposed the "separation of Church and State" of the sectarian Liberals, because in theory and in fact it did not mean separation at all but perhaps the most drastic unification of Church and State which history had known. . Within this "free state" the so-called "free church" was subject to a political control more complete than the Tudor or Stuart or Bourbon monarchies dreamed of. . . . In the system sponsored by sectarian Liberals, as has been said, "the state pretends to ignore the Church: in reality it never took more cognizance of her." In the law of 1905, *the clamactic development*, the Church was

---

in Post-Reformation theory, between civil society and domestic society. The ruler appears in *Libertas* as *paterfamilias,* who is to "govern in kindly fashion and with a sort of fatherly love. In *Immortale Dei* the subjects appear as children, who are 'to be obedient to their rulers and show them reverence and loyalty, with a certain species of that *pietas* which children show their parents.' In this paternal conception of rule, the power of the ruler extends to a care of the total welfare of his children subjects, the illiterate masses. His *patria potestas* is to protect them, since they cannot protect themselves, in their possession of the patrimony of Christian truth that has been their heritage in the traditionally Catholic nation. To this end the ruler is to repress the 'offenses of the unbridled mind' which are like 'injuries violently wrought upon the weak' (*Libertas*)."

[66] "*Leo XIII and Contemporary Theology,*" *Leo XIII and the Modern World,* ed. E. T. Gargan (New York: Sheed and Ward, 1961), p. 225; "Leo by training conceived government as a paternalistic function."

[67] "The Life and Work of Leo XIII," *Leo XIII and the Modern World,* p. 43: "Leo thought of government in paternalistic terms. For this reason he permitted broad powers in the regulation of the lives of the citizens. Here too his own experience was determinative, and his thoughts on liberty must be studied against this background."

[68] Regan, p. 49.

> arrogantly assigned a judicial statute articulating in forty-five articles whereby almost every aspect of her organization and action was minutely regulated. Moreover, this was done on the principle—the principle of primacy of the political, the principle of "everything within the state, nothing above the state."
> . . . This thesis was utterly rejected by the founders of the American Republic. . . . The American thesis is that government is not juridically omnipotent; its powers are limited, one of the principles of limitations is the distinction between state and church.[69]

It would appear, therefore, since the Leonine union of Church and State is necessary to preclude the deification of secular authority, that such a union would not be demanded in the United States. Neither the freedom nor the existence of the Church is jeopardized by the American experience of democracy. Moreover, the necessity of a formal union between Church and State called for by Pope Leo need not therefore be obligatory in every form of political experience. When the duty of acknowledging God is met by society at large the terms of Pope Leo's pronouncements are fulfilled. The United States does in fact through its various societies profess the worship of God.

Article 3. Pope Pius XII (1939-1958)

Pope Pius XII adopted the juridical concept of the State as only one order of action within the framework of society.

> Man as such is by no means to be considered the object of social life or a sort of inert element in it; on the contrary, he is the subject, the foundation and the end of social life.[70]

Society is vastly changed in the thought of Pius XII. The state is not the Leonine paternalistic entity. Society is not reformed from head down to the citizen. The citizen is not the child of the civil

[69] Murray, "The Problem of Pluralism in America," *Thought*, XXIX (1954), 199-200.

[70] Pius XII, *Radio message*, 24 December 1944—*AAS* (1945), 12.

ruler. Rather the citizen is the subject and foundation of the society. He is an individual who needs not to look to a more enlightened clique to supply his wants. The state, then, for Pius XII is structured from the bottom up. The chief function of the state is to protect the individual's inviolable rights. Government has the task of watching itself so that each citizen is free to fulfill his own proper destiny.[71]

In connection with this changed view of society Pope Pius extolled political and civil toleration. The Pontiff declared that not only was tolerance permissible, it was also a moral duty.

> The increasingly frequent contacts between different professions, mingled indiscriminately within the same nation, have caused civil authorities to follow the principles of "tolerance" and "liberty of conscience." In fact, there is a political tolerance, a civil tolerance, a social tolerance, in regard to adherents of other religious beliefs which, in circumstances such as these, is a moral duty for Catholics.[72]

The Pontiff's statement indicated that there was no necessity to disregard the religious convictions of non-Catholic fellow citizens. The Pontiff made this fact known in his address to the Fifth National Convention of the Union of Italian Catholic Jurists.[73] In this address the Pope outlined the basic Catholic position towards religious toleration in the international community. But the principles of the address are equally applicable to the national political experience.[74]

The principles announced by the Pontiff can be characterized under the following headings:

> 1. Above all, it must be clearly stated that no human authority, no state, no community of states, whatever be their religious character, can give a positive command or positive authorization to teach or to do that which

[71] Pius XII, *Radio message,* 1 June 1941—*AAS,* XXXIII (1941), 200.

[72] Pius XII, *Allocution,* "Address to the Roman Rota," *AAS,* XXXIX (1947), 494; translation from the *Clergy Review,* XXIX (1948), 197.

[73] *AAS, XLV* (1953), 794-82; translation from *The Pope Speaks,* I (1954), 64-71.

[74] Regan, p. 62.

> would be contrary to religious truth or moral good.[75]
> 2. Reality shows that error and sin are in the world in great measure. God reprobates them, but He permits them to exist. Hence the affirmation: religious and moral error must always be impeded when it is possible, because toleration of them is itself immoral, is not valid *absolutely and unconditionally.*[76]
> 3. The duty of repressing moral and religious error cannot therefore be an ultimate norm of action. It must be subordinate to *higher and more general* norms, which in some circumstances permit, and even perhaps seem to indicate as the better policy toleration of error in order to promote a greater good.[77]

Without specifying what the concrete higher norms are, the Pope admits that such norms do govern the relations of religious belief within the state. Certainly the tranquillity of the social order is the highest good of every political activity. Human activity demands the stable, peaceful society if man is to prosper. It would appear that the common good of the citizens would be one such example of the "higher and more general norms" enunciated by the Holy Father. Since this is so, the American solution of Church-State relations, wherein the liberty of the Church and its consequent right to preach, is guaranteed, assuredly can be accepted as in harmony with the teachings of Pope Pius XII.

The Pope closed his address with a repudiation of a "complete separation of the two powers of the Church and State."[78] As has been noted, the American version of democracy never separated the two spheres as did the "liberal" movement of Europe. The present constitutional construction of the *Schempp* case[79] is one of neutrality, not of indifferentism or of hostility.

Article 4. Pope John XXIII (1958-1963)

The Constitution of the United States seems in conformity with the papal doctrine enunciated by Pope John XXIII in his Encyc-

---

[75] *The Pope Speaks,* I, 67.

[76] *The Pope Speaks,* I, 68.

[77] *The Pope Speaks,* I, 68.

[78] *The Pope Speaks,* I, 71.

[79] *School District of Abington Township v. Schempp,* 374 U.S. 203, 83 S. Ct. 1560, 10 L. Ed. 2d. 844; supra, pp. 119-122.

lical, *Pacem in Terris.*[80] Pope John states in this great message that each man has as a natural endowment the right to worship his Creator according to the dictates of his own conscience.

> . . . This too must be listed among the rights of a human being, to honor God according to the sincere dictates of his conscience, and therefore the right to practice his religion privately and publicly. For as Lactantius so clearly taught: *We were created for the purpose of showing to the God Who bore us the submission we owe Him, of recognizing Him alone, and of serving Him. We are obliged and bound* by this duty to God: from this religion itself *receives its name.* And on this point Our Predecessor of immortal memory, Leo XIII, declared: *This genuine, this honorable freedom of the sons of God, which most nobly protects the dignity of the human person, is greater than any violence or injustice; it has always been sought by the Church, and always most dear to her. This was the freedom which the Apostles claimed with intrepid constancy, which the apologists defended with their writings, and which the martyrs in such numbers consecrated with their blood.*[81]

Article 5. Decree of II Vatican Council

The collected bishops of the Roman Catholic Church called by Pope John to the Second Vatican Council reaffirmed the statements of Pope John XXIII in their decree on religious freedom. The fathers of the Council proclaimed the Catholic belief that all men have as their natural human right the power to worship God as their conscience best dictates.

> This Vatican Council declares that the human person has a right to religious freedom. This freedom means that all men are to be immune from coercion on the part of individuals or of social groups, and of any human power, in such ways that no one is to be forced to act in a manner contrary to his own beliefs, whether pri-

[80] *AAS,* LV (1963), 257-304; translation: National Catholic Welfare Conference (Washington, D. C.).

[81] *Pacem in Terris,* n. 14.

> vately or publicly, whether alone or in association with others, within due limits.[82]

Not only do individuals have the natural right of professing God as they see Him, but the Council also declared that religious societies and communities, "provided the just demands of public order are observed,"[83] enjoy the same rights. Religious societies are a requirement of the social nature of men and of religion.[84] They must therefore be guaranteed the right to govern themselves, to preach their doctrines, both to members and non-members, and to freely conduct their meetings without legal restrictions from the secular society.[85]

The II Vatican Council declared that the protection of the rights of citizens and religious groups formed by them to religious freedom is an essential duty of government.

> Therefore the care of the right to religious freedom devolves upon the whole citizenry, upon social groups, upon government, and upon the church and other religious communities, in virtue of the duty of all toward the common welfare, and in the manner proper to each.
>
> The protection and promotion of the inviolable rights of man ranks among the essential duties of government. Therefore government is to assume the safeguard of the religious freedom of all its citizens, in an effective manner, by just laws and by other appropriate means.[86]

The Council fathers realized that religion can be used by people for other than the most worthy of motives. They recognized that religious rights are exercised in a human and cultural society. Men must practice religious freedom with due regard

---

[82] *Declaratio De Libertate Religiosa De Iure Personae et Communicatum ad Libertatem Socialem et Civilem in re Religiosa,* December 11, 1965; N.C.W.C. translation.

[83] *Op. cit.,* n. 4.

[84] *Loc. cit.*

[85] *Op. cit.,* n. 4.

[86] *Op. cit.,* n. 6.

for the rights of others and in accordance with the principles of the moral law. The society

> . . has the right to defend itself against possible abuses committed on the pretext of freedom of religion. It is the special duty of government to provide this protection.[87]

It would seem that the best method for ensuring the proper protection of religious freedom and insuring the good of the society would be to guarantee these rights constitutionally.

> Consequently, in order that relationships of peace and harmony be established and maintained within the whole of mankind, it is necessary that religious freedom be everywhere provided with an effective constitutional guarantee and that respect be shown for the high duty and right of man freely to lead his religious life in society.[88]

Following the statements of Pope John XXIII and the II Vatican Council each citizen should look to some legal provision to ensure that as an individual and as a member of a religious group his religious liberties should be constitutionally guaranteed. This right in fact is secured in the United States through the "free exercise" and the "establishment" clauses of the First Amendment. The effect of these clauses provides that the individual and the religious groups comprising society are insured that government will and must act neutrally towards all the members of the political community.[89]

---

[87] *Op. cit.,* n. 7.

[88] *Op. cit.,* n. 15.

[89] *School District of Abington Township v. Schempp,* 374 U.S. 203, 83 S. Ct. 1560, 10 L. Ed. 2d. 844.

CHAPTER IV

The Tenure of Church Property

SECTION 1. CANONICAL LEGISLATION ON CHURCH PROPERTY

Article 1. Introduction

Every society of human beings has need of material means to attain its own goals. In a differentiated and universal society composed of various officials, departments, and varied functions such as the Church, the use of temporal means is absolutely imperative. The Catholic Church as a perfect divinely constituted public society[1] has the need to own and to use property to fulfill its divine mandate.

The Church has the right to demand support from the faithful to supply its physical requirements. This right of the Church is independent of any civil authority and it extends to the goods necessary for the maintenance of the clergy, for the conduct of divine worship, and for whatever ends the Church was established to serve.[2] The faithful's obligation of support is grounded on both the natural law and the positive divine law. The Church has the obligation of praying for, instructing, ministering to, and offering the divine services for mankind. Correlatively, each member of the Church is bound by the natural law to render financial support for Church assistance in the work of salvation. The binding force of the natural law obligation is confirmed by the positive divine law. When Christ sent forth His disciples, He instructed them to depend on the people to whom they were preaching for sustenance and clothing.[3] Christ also approved the Judaic law which demanded support for religion through the payment of dues for the Temple.[4] Although He maintained that neither He nor His Apostles were

---

[1] *Supra*, pp. 25-26.

[2] *CIC.*, can. 1496; *Postquam*, can. 233.

[3] Matthew, 10: 9-10.

[4] Matthew, 17: 23-26.

bound by that law, the fact that He insisted on their freedom from the law indicates His approval of the law as binding upon all who were not called to devote themselves to the specific works of religion.[5]

Article 2. The Structure of the Church

The Catholic Church and the Apostolic See have the native right freely and independently of any civil power to acquire, own and administer temporal property in the prosecution of the ends for which they have been established.[6] The right of the Church to own property follows from the fact of its divine establishment in the nature of a moral personality.[7] The Church maintains that the right to own property is its native right (*nativum ius*), i.e., a right which emanates from the nature and essence of the society. Hence, once the Church had been established as a visible society, it is impossible for it not to have the right to acquire temporal goods.[8]

It cannot be too strongly pointed out that the right of the Church to own and administer its possessions does not flow from the beneficence of the civil authority. Both the Church and the State are perfect societies, and consequently the State has no power to arbitrarily impose limitations which postulate the Church's existence as amenable to the civil institutions. Christ in founding His Church did not subject it to civil authority. Rather,

> . . Christ willed that His Church should not depend even indirectly upon the State. This indirect dependence would manifest itself if the purpose and end of the ecclesiastical society—free and independent in its own

---

[5] Kremer, *Church Support in the United States,* The Catholic University of America Canon Law Studies, n. 61 (Washington, D. C.: The Catholic University of America, 1930), pp. 38-39.

[6] *CIC.,* can. 1495, § 1; *Postquam,* can. 232, § 1.

[7] *CIC.,* can. 100, § 1; *Cler. Sanc.,* can. 28, § 1.

[8] Goodwine, *The Right of the Church to Acquire Temporal Goods,* The Catholic University of America Canon Law Studies, n. 131 (Washington, D. C.: The Catholic University of America Press, 1941), pp. 2-3 (hereafter cited Goodwine).

> order—were found to be subject to and subordinate to the purpose and end of the civil society. . . . From this it must be clear that Christ's evident will was that His Church be absolutely independent of civil society. As such, it is impossible that the Church depend upon civil society for the very means for its end, viz. the right to acquire and administer temporal goods.[9]

The Church accomplishes its mission through the establishment of subordinate moral personalities as its effective instruments. These moral personalities are the creatures of the Church and receive their existence through ecclesiastical constitution and recognition.[10] The moral personalities established by the law of the Church have the right of acquiring, owning and administering property in conformity with the sacred canons.[11] These ecclesiastical societies receive their juridic personality from the general laws of the Church and are therefore subject to the restrictions imposed upon them by the central authority.

The Patriarchates have the right to own property. The property in the form of gifts, inheritances, legacies, alms and offerings may be accepted by the Patriarchs and are to be used in accordance with the wishes of the donors.[12]

Dioceses in like manner have the right to own and administer property granted to them. Through their erection, reserved to the Holy See,[13] dioceses are constituted as non-collegiate moral personalities. In virtue of canon 1495, § 2, they may own and administer property in their own names.

Ordinaries in their own dioceses have the right to establish benefices, such as parishes.[14] These parishes as moral personalities partake in the right to own and acquire property as deriving through the prescriptions of the sacred canons.[15]

Religious houses, provinces and religious institutions have the

---

[9] Goodwine, p. 47.

[10] *CIC.*, cans. 99, 100, § 1; *Cler. Sanc.*, cans. 27 and 28, § 1.

[11] *CIC.*, can. 1495, § 2; *Postquam*, can. 232, § 2.

[12] *Cler. Sanc.*, can. 261, § 1; *Postquam*, can. 232, § 2.

[13] *CIC.*, can. 248, § 2; *Cler. Sanc.*, can. 194, § 2.

[14] *CIC.*, can. 1414, § 2.

[15] *CIC.*, can. 1495, § 2.

right to own and acquire temporalities. Sometimes the rules or constitutions of a particular institute restrain or exclude the right to own or acquire religious goods.[16] However, such limitations are placed on the institute by the Church, which itself gives the institute existence[17] and establishes the rules of operation for the group.[18]

The Church establishes hospitals, orphanages, schools and other similar institutions dedicated to the works of religion or the execution of the spiritual or corporal works of charity. Such institutions normally may be erected by the local ordinary;[19] however, the erection of Catholic Universities is reserved for the approval of the Holy See.[20] These institutions are non-collegiate moral personalities. They have the right to obtain and own property in conformity with the general prescriptions of ownership of ecclesiastical property, as stated in canon 1495, § 2.

Article 3. Acquisition of Church Property

It has already been stated that the Church and subsidiary moral personalities established by the Church are entitled to support in accordance with both the natural and the positive divine laws. The modes in which ownership is acquired emanate from both the natural law and the positive law. The Church may acquire goods in either of these ways.[21] The valid means of acquiring property and rights as flowing from the natural law are occupation, accession and labor. However, the civil law may set prescriptions for the obtaining of ownership in its domain. Canon 1529 recognizes the right of the State to determine standards for the valid execution of civil contracts. The law stated in canon 1529 requires that whatever the civil law of a country demands in relation to contracts and payments of all kinds is also by the Canon Law to be observed in ecclesiastical matters, and has the same effects. The

---

[16] *CIC.*, can. 531; *Postquam,* can. 63, § 1.
[17] *CIC.*, can. 100, § 1; *Cler. Sanc.,* can. 28, § 1.
[18] *CIC.*, can. 492.
[19] *CIC.*, can. 1489, § 1.
[20] *CIC.*, can. 1376, § 1.
[21] *CIC.*, can. 1499, § 1; *Postquam,* can. 236, § 1.

only limitation set by the law in question looks to such civil laws which are contrary to the divine law or to the rules enacted in Canon Law. This exception flows from the vindication of the right of the Church to own property. If the civil law would declare that the Church, in the light of its nature, may in no way be admitted into commercial transactions, there would be an implicit denial of the natural and positive divine right of the Church to acquire property. Such a denial would exceed the rights of any civil power, since the Church exists by divine will to the abstraction of any and all vindication from civil authority.

Ecclesiastical law expressly prohibits the operation of legal prescription with reference to the following rights and goods:

1. those of the natural or positive divine law;
2. those spiritual rights which lay persons are incapable of acquiring, if there is question of a prescription in favor of lay persons;
3. those which can be obtained only by Apostolic privilege;
4. the certified and undisputed boundary lines of ecclesiastical provinces, dioceses, parishes, vicariates and prefectures apostolic, abbacies and prelacies *nullius;*
5. stipends and obligations connected with Masses;
6. ecclesiastical benefices without title;
7 the right of visitation and obedience, if this would entail that the subjects cannot be visited by any prelate and are no longer subject to any prelate;
8. the payment of the *cathedraticum.*[22]

Aside from these forms of invalid prescriptions, the Church adopts as its own the civil law of prescription as found in the country.[23]

The Oriental Law makes specific provision that the goods of ecclesiastical moral personalities should be held in accordance with the civil enactments if public moral personalities as established by the Church are not civilly recognized. The superiors of these

---

[22] *CIC.*, can. 1509; *Postquam,* can. 247.

[23] *CIC.*, can. 1508; *Postquam,* can. 246, § 1.

moral personalities, be they religious or secular, are obliged to consult civil lawyers to find the best form of ownership to insure the valid civil administration of ecclesiastical goods. The superiors are further obligated to secure the opinion of the board of administrators over and above the advice of civil lawyers.[24]

In the acquisition of temporal goods by ecclesiastical personalities the laws respecting their ownership are seen to be an accommodation of Canon Law to the rules of civil law. Although the Church maintains the native right to own and administer its own properties, the accommodations to civil law show the earnest charity of the Church to maintain the requirements of civil harmony in whatever country it functions.

Prior to the promulgation of the present Code of Canon Law, there was considerable controversy regarding the proper subject of ownership of ecclesiastical goods.[25] The dominion of ecclesiastical temporalities is now determined by canon 1499, § 2, of the Code of Canon Law. This enactment declares that the ownership of goods vests in the moral personality acquiring the goods. The moral personalities, however, must acquire them in conformity with the norms of the sacred canons.

Article 4. Administration of Church Property

The Roman Pontiff is the supreme dispenser and administrator of all ecclesiastical properties in virtue of his office.[26] The expression of the law follows the position held by Saint Thomas Aquinas (1225-1274), who observed that ecclesiastical properties belong to the Pope as the principal dispenser of such goods rather than as their owner or possessor.[27] The Pontiff administers the prop-

---

[24] *Postquam,* can. 256, § 2.

[25] Cf. Navarrus, *Opera Omnia* (6 vols., Venetiis, 1618), II, 515 ff. Suarez (*Opera Omnia* [28 vols. in 30, Parisiis, 1856-78], Tom. 24, p. 443) maintained that the proper owner of ecclesiastical property was God Himself.

[26] *CIC.,* can. 1518; *Postquam,* can. 257; cf. Comyns, *Papal and Episcopal Administration of Church Property,* The Catholic University of America Canon Law Studies, n. 147 (Washington, D. C.: The Catholic University of America, 1942), pp. 57 ff.

[27] *Summa Theologica* (5 vols., Taurini, Marietti, 1932), IIa, IIae, q. 100, a. 1, ad 7.

erty of the Holy See through the offices and officials of the Roman Curia.[28]

Since moral personalities are held equal to minors in the law,[29] they must perforce act through administrators who themselves are subject to the provisions of law. The local ordinary is the guardian of the ecclesiastical goods of his diocese. His is not the task of administering such goods, but of supervising the proper administration of all temporalities within his jurisdiction.[30] In Oriental eparchies there is established the office of econome whose task it is to supervise the goods of moral personalities within the eparchy acting as the agent of the patriarch or the hierarch.[31]

The ordinary is neither the supreme administrator in the sense in which the Pope is, nor is he the primary administrator of the goods of the moral personalities. The bishop must set up norms for the administration of the goods of the moral personalities within his jurisdiction, which norms must not conflict with the Church's universal law.[32] However, with due regard for the rights of individuals, for the legitimate customs in force within his domain, and for the special conditions obtaining in his territory, the ordinary establishes such rules as will facilitate the greatest protection and the most secure management of the ecclesiastical goods under his supervision. It is most opportune that the rules for the management of the financial interests of the Church within a diocese be regulated by statutes promulgated as diocesan statutes at the time of the synods.[33]

To assist the bishop in the proper custody of the goods of the diocese, there is need for him to found in his episcopal city a council of administrators, consisting of the ordinary, as president, and of two or more qualified men, who should within what is possible be familiar also with the civil law. The members of this board are to be appointed by the bishop after consulting with the

---

[28] Abbo-Hannan, II, p. 724.

[29] *CIC.*, can. 100, § 3; *Cler. Sanc.*, can. 28, § 3.

[30] *CIC.*, can. 1519, § 1.

[31] *Postquam,* cans. 262, 251, § 1.

[32] *CIC.*, 1519, § 2.

[33] Augustine, VI, 579.

diocesan consultors, unless some other equivalent provision has already been legitimately made by special law or custom.[34]

The local bishop is to receive each year a financial report from all administrators, both clerics and lay, of all churches, pious places, and religious and charitable institutions as well as all confraternities.[35]

In addition to his duties as the custodian or guardian of ecclesiastical properties, the bishop is the proper administrator of the goods belonging to the diocese as such and to the *mensa episcopalis,* i.e., the benefice of the diocese granting financial support to the bishop.[36] The bishop in the matter of the episcopal benefice is held accountable to the Sacred Consistorial Congregation for his own proper administration of the benefice entrusted to his charge.[37]

Pastors are bound to act as the proper administrators of the goods of their parishes.[38] They are obliged to make an annual report of the funds of the parish to the bishop.[39] Any loss sustained by the moral personality committed to their charge as a result of their negligence or culpability must be restored from their own personal funds.[40]

Religious supervisors are the administrators of the goods of their institutes, houses and provinces. They must function in conformity with the rules of their constitutions as well as the universal law of the Church.[41] Expenditures and legal acts of ordinary administration can be validly performed not only by the superiors, but also within the limits of their office by the officials, designated for those purposes by the constitutions of the respective institutes.[42]

---

[34] *CIC.,* can. 1520, § 1.
[35] *CIC.,* can. 1525; *Postquam,* can. 269.
[36] *CIC.,* can. 349, § 2, n. 1.
[37] *CIC.,* can. 248, § 3.
[38] *CIC.,* can. 1476, § 1; *Postquam,* can. 264, § 2, n. 3.
[39] *CIC.,* can. 1525; *Postquam,* can. 269.
[40] *CIC.,* can. 1476, § 2.
[41] *CIC.,* can. 532, § 1; *Postquam,* can. 64, § 1.
[42] *CIC.,* can. 532, § 2; *Postquam,* can. 64, § 2.

In the investment of funds the local ordinary must be consulted in the following cases:

1. by the superioress of nuns and of diocesan congregations for the investment of money; if the monastery of nuns is subject to a regular superior, his consent is required as well;
2. by the superioress of congregations of papal approval, if the money to be invested is the dowry of professed sisters;
3. by the superioress or superior of a house of any religious congregation if the funds or the goods have been donated or bequeathed to the religious house for divine worship or for the works of charity to be carried on in the same place;
4. by any religious, even of an exempt order, if the money was given to a parish or a mission, or to the religious for the benefit of the parish or the mission.[43]

These rules are applicable also for changes of investments, and not only for the initial investments of the funds.[44]

The superiors or administrators of moral personalities instituted for the works of religion or for the administration of the spiritual or corporal works of the Church are bound to faithfully execute the rules of the foundation of such institutions. The rector of any institute is bound by the same obligations and enjoys the same rights as the administrator of other ecclesiastical goods enjoys.[45] The rectors accordingly must make an annual report to the bishop, and all customs to contrary are reprobated.[46]

All administrators of the goods of the Church are to regard their entrusted task as a sacred charge. They must imitate the cautious policy of the prudent householder in their solicitude for the temporalities entrusted to them. As such, they must

1. guard against any loss or damage to the ecclesiastical goods confided to their care;

---

[43] *CIC.*, can. 533, § 1.

[44] *CIC.*, can. 533, § 2.

[45] *CIC.*, can. 1489.

[46] *CIC.*, can. 1492, § 1.

2. observe the rules of both canon and civil law, and the special regulations imposed by the founder or donor or the legitimate authority;
3. collect the revenues and income of the goods diligently and at the proper time, keep them in a safe place, and expend them according to the intention of the founder or the existing laws and regulations;
4. invest the surplus revenue of a church, with the consent of the ordinary, for the benefit of the church;
5. keep the records of receipts and expenditures in good order;
6. arrange and keep, in the archives or in a suitable and proper place, the documents and papers on which the property rights of the church are based; authentic copies of these papers should, whenever it can be conveniently done, be kept also in the archives or safe of the diocesan curia.[47]

SECTION 2. TENURE OF PROPERTY IN AMERICAN CIVIL LAW

Article 1. Introduction

The Catholic Church in American civil law is considered a private religious society. The Church's right to establish ecclesiastical moral personalities is recognized, but they do not attain civil corporate status thereby. Ecclesiastical moral personalities founded by the Church remain merely religious societies.

The American civil law upholds and protects the right of citizens to join a church and to hold property for the benefit of that religious organization. In *Watson v. Jones*[48] the Supreme Court of the United States declared:

> In this country the full and free right to entertain any religious belief, to practice any religious doctrine which does not violate the laws of morality and property, and which does not infringe personal rights, is conceded to all. The law knows no heresy, and is committed to the support of no dogma, the establishment of no sect. The right to organize voluntary religious associations to assist in the expression and dissemination of any religious

---

[47] *CIC.*, can. 1525; *Postquam,* can. 269.

[48] *Watson v. Jones,* 80 U.S. 679, 20 L. Ed. 666 (1871).

> doctrine, and to create tribunals for the decision of controverted questions of faith within the association, and for the ecclesiastical government of all the individual members, congregations, and officers within the general association, is unquestioned.[49]

The Supreme Court in this ruling evidences two important factors in the civil law view of religious organizations. The unquestioned right to worship God in conformity with the dictates of one's conscience is affirmed. The Court also recognizes that the religious association of necessity must hold property to secure the goals of the religious society. It distinguishes in the opinion three general classifications of property held by the religious association. The first class of property is held in trust for the support of a specific dogma or form of religious worship. The second class of property is that holding which is held by a congregation that has no immediate superior. The third is that which is held by a local church that is subject to a higher form of ecclesiastical government, whether it be a body as it is called in the presbyterian system or whether it be a religious superior duly constituted in his hierarchical or prelatial rank or standing. But in whatever mode the ecclesiastical body secures property, it has the right to so maintain it.

The Roman Catholic Church is viewed in American civil law as one of many religious societies. A religious society has been defined by American law as a body of believers professing the same creed under a common authority and practicing the same religious practices.[50] The Courts have agreed that a voluntary religious society is formed for the advancement of the spiritual welfare of its members, by counsel, admonition and example, and with a view to enabling the society to pay a pastor to look after the welfare of the particular organization and its charitable endeavors and to promote, as far as possible, with the means at its disposal, the welfare of the race.[51]

---

[49] *Loc. cit.*

[50] *Baptist Church v. Witherell,* 11 N.Y. 296 (1832).

[51] *Scott Co. v. Roman Catholic Archbishop, Diocese of Oregon,* 83 Ore. 97, 163 P. 88 (1917); *Jones v. State,* 28 Neb. 495, 44 N.W. 658 (1890).

Civil practice recognizes a triple understanding of the term religious association. Jurisprudence distinguishes congregation, church, and ecclesiastical corporation, if there be one, since it is not necessary to incorporate. This distinction was first drawn in *Miller v. Baptist Church.*[52] The term "congregation" embraces all the persons of a religious society in the act of worship. The congregation is not the fixed body of believers. It is a variable group of persons gathered to worship. Their justapositioning at a religious service does not mean that each person fully accepts the totality of the doctrine of the persuasion.

In opposition to the "congregation," "church" has the legal connotation of the body of worshippers who fully embrace the totality of the doctrine and bind themselves to the internal discipline of the group. The continuance of membership in a church is predicated upon fidelity of the communicant to the rules of the society.

> When they became members, they did so on the condition of continuing or not as themselves and the church might determine. In that respect, they voluntarily subject themselves to the ecclesiastical power and cannot invoke the supervision or control of that jurisdiction by this or any other civil court.[53]

The same construction of church membership was enunciated by the Supreme Court in *Watson v. Jones:*

> All who unite themselves to such a body [religious society] do so with the implied consent to this government, and are bound to submit to it,[54]

and again in *Hundley v. Collins.*[55]

The "corporation" in relation to the religious society is

> . . . the legal entity which holds title to the real and personal estate used for worship or other religious purposes

---

[52] *Miller v. Baptist Church,* 16 N.J.L. 251 (1837).

[53] *Shannon v. Frost,* 42 Ky. 253 (1842).

[54] *Watson v. Jones,* 80 U.S. 679, 20 L. Ed. 666.

[55] *Hundley v. Collins,* 131 Ala. 234, 32 S. 575 (1902).

> in the absence of express provision to the contrary. . . . The corporation and church, although indissolubly associated, were nevertheless separated by this distinct line of demarcation.[56]

It was necessary for churches to incorporate because they are unable to be recognized in civil law in their public character as subsidiary moral personalities created by the Roman Catholic Church. Further the law of incorporations is directly opposed to recognizing as public the moral personalities established by the Church. English common law espoused the so-called Concession Theory of Corporations.

> The corporation is, and must be, the creature of the state. Into its nostrils the state must breathe the breath of fictitious life, for otherwise it would be no animated body, but individualistic dust.[57]

Each religious society is free to maintain the property interests it has in whatever form that is deemed best by and for each group. The civil authorities are not to impose on any religious society the means for holding property. In a Missouri decision the court ruled

> Sometimes it will be useful for churches to incorporate in order to transact their secular affairs conveniently, and the wiser policy would permit them to do so without depriving the established ecclesiastical authorities of power. Many religious sects, and among them the Roman Catholic, are of world-wide extent and vast membership, with congregations, parishes, and established hierarchies and councils in every land. For ages they have observed a uniform policy, not only in spiritual matters, but in the transactions of secular business and the management

---

[56] *McNeilly v. First Presbyterian Church of Brookline,* 243 Mass. 331, 137 N.E. 691 (1923).

[57] Gierke-Maitland, *Political Theories of the Middle Ages* (Cambridge, 1900), Translator's Introduction, p. xxx; Blackstone, *Commentaries on the Laws of England* (4 vols., New York, 1852), I, 472 (hereafter cited Blackstone).

> of properties. To force upon them an unaccustomed economy would introduce confusion and embarrassment; whereas to refuse them corporate capacity, except on condition of renouncing their customs, would be illiberal treatment of the state.[58]

The court in this decision saw incorporation as but one method of holding property open to a religious society. The society, then, is free to choose that form of tenure that best suits its individual needs.

The Holy See through the Congregation of the Council in 1911 issued the following directive regarding the tenure of ecclesiastical property in the United States.

> 1. Among the methods which are now in use in the United States for holding and administering church property, the one known as *Parish Corporation* is preferable to the others, but with the conditions and safeguards which are now in use in the State of New York. The Bishops therefore should immediately take steps to introduce this method for the handling of property in their diocese, if the civil law allows it. If the civil law does not allow it, they should exert their influence with the civil authorities that it may be made legal as soon as possible.
> 2. Only in those places where civil law does not recognize *Parish Corporation,* and until such recognition is obtained, the method commonly called *Corporation Sole* is allowed, but with the understanding that in the administration of ecclesiastical property the Bishop is to act with the advice, and in more important matters with the consent, of those who have an interest in the premises and of the diocesan consultors, this being a conscientious obligation for the Bishop in person.
> 3. The method called in *fee simple* is to be entirely abandoned.[59]

---

[58] *Klix v. Polish Roman Catholic St. Stanislaus Parish,* 137 Mo. App. 347, 118 S.W. 1171 (1901).

[59] *Canon Law Digest,* edited by T. Lincoln Bouscaren and James I. O'Connor (5 vols., Milwaukee: Bruce Publishing Co., Vol. I, 1934; Vol. II, 1943; Vol. III, 1954; Vol. IV, 1958; Vol. V, 1963), II, 444-445.

Article 2. Fee Simple

Fee simple is a form of tenure of property. Fee simple conveys an absolute and direct ownership of the property. More precisely, fee simple is not a form of tenure; it is rather a degree of estate.[60] A tenant in fee simple is one who has lands, tenements, or hereditaments to hold for himself and for his heirs forever; generally absolutely and simply; all mention of the heirs remaining a matter for his own good pleasure, or looking to specific dispositions of the law.[61]

The decree of the Congregation of the Council expressly prohibits the holding of church property in fee simple. The reason for the condemnation is obvious. The bishop as the holder of ecclesiastical properties could fail to enact a proper transfer to his successor in office. In that event the church temporalities and rights would pass to the bishop's heirs and be lost to the ecclesiastical purposes for which the property was given. The courts in such a case would declare that an implied trust was involved in the bishop's holdings, the bishop acting as the trustee of ecclesiastical properties, but this would necessitate extended civil litigation needlessly.

Article 3. Trustees

> In Ohio at the present time charitable and benevolent institutions under the ownership, control and management of religious communities belonging to the Catholic Church are separately incorporated and therefore hold their property in that manner. Although the Catholic dioceses may incorporate . . . *de facto* they are unincorporated and as such are without the capacity to hold title to property. These unincorporated societies enjoy the benefits of property by means of trust tenure.[62]

A trust is defined as the right of property held by one person,

---

[60] Blackstone, II, 103.

[61] Blackstone, II, 104.

[62] Wiggins, *Property Laws of the State of Ohio Affecting the Church*, The Catholic University of America Canon Law Studies, n. 367 (Washington, D. C.: The Catholic University of America Press, 1956), pp. 75-76.

called the trustee, for the benefit of another person, called the beneficiary or *cestui que trust*.[63] The system of trust tenure arose from the use of property based on a fiduciary relationship given to a person for the benefit of a third party. The legal title vests in the trustee and the equitable title vests in the *cestui que trust*.

The courts, in exercising their jurisprudence, have described and defined trusts. They have regarded them with favor and have brought grounds to support them. A trust is described as a creature of equity. The trust comes into being when the title to property is conferred upon, and accepted by, one person on the terms of holding, using, or disposing of it for the benefit of another. A trust is in the nature of the disposition by which the proprietor cedes to another party property with which he is entrusted. The property is to be used for the needs of a third party. A trust is the right, enforceable in equity, to the beneficial enjoyment of property, the legal title of which is in another. The person creating the trust is designated as the "settlor," "donor" or "trustor." He to whom the title of property is given in trust and in whom the legal title vests is called the trustee. The person for whose benefit the trust has been established is called the beneficiary. The property entrusted is received under the name of the *trust res* or subject matter. The basic idea of a trust is this separate coexistence of the legal title with the beneficial ownership or, as it came to be called, the equitable title.

The relationship which arises in the creation of the trust is called fiduciary inasmuch as one party trusts his property or interest to the dominion of another and relies upon the integrity of that other party to do nothing that would impair the interest confided in him. A trust often will not be valid unless it is recognizable and enforceable in the courts. The courts of equity will not create the trusts because they are not empowered to establish fiduciary relationships. The courts, however, will uphold and enforce a trust if there is proof adequate to sustain the existence of a trust.

An express trust must be created by the settlor. If he is *sui iuris* he may create an express trust by an *inter vivos* declaration,

[63] Bouvier, *Law Dictionary* (2 vols., Boston, 1897), II, 1144.

deed, or enforceable agreement, or by a testamentary disposition, or by an effective creation of an imperative power.

If an owner of property who is *sui iuris* wishes to declare that he holds such property in trust for another, he may do so either orally or in writing. The declaration must be a completely executed transaction complying with the requirements of consideration, and it will thus have the effect of creating a trust immediately. The intention to become a trustee must be clearly expressed.

It is impossible to have a trust without a *trust res*. A trust must always be created with respect to property. Anything which has economic or exchange value is usually proper subject matter for the creation of a trust. It must be transferable, in actual existence, and ascertainable at the time of the creation of the trust.

The trustee is required to take an estate or interest in the *trust res* sufficient in extent to enable him to exercise the powers and duties imposed upon him in the administration of the trust. The settlor's intention is the controlling view in this respect. Usually in the deed or will, an estate or title is conveyed or transferred to the trustee. If the instrument creating the trust confers upon the trustee mandatory powers but fails to transfer any estate to him there will be implied an estate sufficient to enable the trustee to carry out the powers given to him. Two qualifications, then, are usually necessary in any trustee. He must be capable to receive and hold the title to property, real or personal, and he must have the business capacity to carry on the management of the trust.

Since the trustee holds property entirely for the benefit of others, the law binds him with the duty of administering the trust most scrupulously in the interests of the beneficiary. This duty is referred to as the trustee's duty of loyalty. Thus the law provides that the trustee has no interest in the property which his own creditors can reach by execution, by proceedings, in bankruptcy, or by any other means.

In the administration of the trust, the trustee is bound to exercise that degree of care and skill which an ordinarily prudent man would exercise in dealing with his own property. Upon the acceptation of the trust, the trustee will prepare an inventory of the goods placed in his care and maintain a careful account of his acts of administration. He is bound to see that the *trust res* is productive. The failure of the trustee to make proper investments or to fulfill his proper duties will make him liable for any financial loss incurred. In the case of the non-payment of debts to the trust, the trustee is to sue in his own name for the uncollected monies. In the proper management of the trust, he may bring any action necessary to protect or defend such property or to recover possession of such property, or compensation for it, when it has unlawfully been appropriated by someone else.

A classic example of the trust doctrine of church property is found in the case of *Mannix v. Purcell.*[64] John B. Purcell was appointed Bishop of the Diocese of Cincinnati in 1833. His brother, Father Edward Purcell, was placed in charge of the finances of the diocese. Many persons deposited their money with Father Purcell when they became distrustful of the banks following the depression of 1837. He loaned the money out for interest. This financial dealing of paying interest to the depositors from the accruements of loans continued for forty years. During the financial panic of 1878, many investors sought to reclaim their funds. Father Purcell was unable to cover all the deposits, because he had lost great sums in bank failures and uncollected debts. The Archbishop assumed the debt as his own and as an individual, he made an assignment in insolvency of all his own property, excluding property he held in trust for others.

Ecclesiastical property in the Archdiocese was held in fee simple at the time.[65] The creditors brought civil action to force the sale of ecclesiastical properties held by the Archbishop, for they contended that he was the absolute owner. It was further contended that no trust could attach to the property. The Ohio Supreme Court ruled against the plaintiffs when it stated that

> . . . parol evidence may be resorted to in order to engraft a trust upon a title held by deed absolute on its face . . . which in this state has passed beyond the range

---

[64] *Mannix v. Purcell,* 46 Ohio 102 (1888).

[65] Lamott, *History of the Archdiocese of Cincinnati* (New York: Frederick Pustet Co., 1921), pp. 189-191.

of serious discussion; though the proof in such cases should be clear, strong and convincing.[66]

Article 4. Incorporation

The civil law in the United States recognizes the corporate status of only those institutions which have been established by the federal government,[67] or by the states of the union permitting the incorporation of ecclesiastical properties.

Civil law in this country has adopted the concession theory regarding the nature of incorporations. The fictitious nature of the corporation was adopted by American jurisprudence. In the case of *Dartmouth College v. Woodward, N.H.,*[68] Chief Justice Marshall stated the American theory of incorporations when he wrote:

> A corporation is an artificial being, invisible, intangible, and existing only in contemplation of the law. Being the mere creature of law, it possesses only those properties which the charter of its creation confers upon it, either expressly, or as incidental to its very existence. These are such as are supposed best calculated to effect the object for which it was created. Among the most important are immortality, and, if the expression may be allowed, individuality, properties by which a perpetual succession of many persons are considered as the same, and may act as a single individual. They enable a corporation to manage its own affairs, and to hold property without the perplexing intricacies, the hazardous and endless necessity of perpetual conveyances, for the purpose of transmitting it from hand to hand. It is chiefly for the purpose of clothing bodies of men, in succession with these qualities and capacities, that corporations were invented, and are in use. By these means a perpetual succession of individuals are capable of acting for the promotion of the particular object, like one immortal being. But this being does not share in the civil government of the country, unless that be the purpose for which it was created. Its immortality no more confers on it

[66] *Mannix v. Purcell,* 46 Ohio 102.

[67] *Bradfield v. Roberts,* 175 U.S. 291, 20 S. Ct. 121, 44 L. Ed. 168 (1899).

[68] *Dartmouth College v. Woodward, N.H.,* 16 U.S. 518, 4 L. Ed. 629 (1819).

> political power, or a political character, than immortality would confer such power or character on a natural person. It is no more a State instrument, than a natural person exercising the same powers.[69]

In some jurisdictions of this country, corporations are defined by statute or by their respective constitutions.[70]

A corporation as a collection of individuals is something other than the persons composing the legally constituted being. The corporation is a separate legal entity.[71] Founded by law, the corporation possesses only those faculties which are conferred upon it by the state.[72] The precise powers are defined by the respective laws of the state of incorporation. The state's role and powers over the corporation were emphasized in *Marchman v. McCoy Hotel Operating Co.*, wherein it was ruled:

> It is elementary that all the powers, franchises and privileges of a corporation are derived exclusively from the Constitution and statutes.[74]

Article 5. Types of Religious Corporations

In the founding days of the country, religious bodies did not formally incorporate. The simplicity of procedure did not necessitate the adoption of corporate forms, and the settlers saw in the practice some union of Church and State which they opposed. In the everyday life of the churches, the ecclesiastical goals were obtainable without formal governmental recognition as a corporation. Gradually it was realized that incorporation was not a union of Church and State, and that corporate status bestowed on the religious society the privilege of legal entities. Legislatures began

---

[69] *Loc. cit.*

[70] *Sneed v. Tippett,* 114 Okla. 173, 245 P. 40 (1926).

[71] *New Colonial Ice Co. v. Helvering,* 292 U.S. 435, 55 S. Ct. 440, 79 L. Ed. 977 (1934); *In re Mt. Sinai Hospital,* 250 N.Y. 103, 164 N.E. 871 (1928).

[72] *Anderson-Tully Co. v. Gillett Lumber Co.,* 155 Ark. 224, 244 S.W. 26 (1922).

[73] *People v. Alaska Pacific S.S. Co.,* 182 Cal. 202, 187 P. 742 (1920).

[74] *Marchman v. McCoy Hotel Operating Co.,* 21 S.W. 2nd. 552 (1929).

to slowly enact special bills to charter religious societies. When this mode of procedure did not receive universal approval, the state constitutions were amended to provide for religious incorporation. In 1965, all but two states permitted religious societies to avail themselves of some form of corporate existence.[75]

The first development in the history of religious corporations in the United States took place in colonial times with the institution of territorial parishes. These parishes were an instrument of the government in colonies having an established religion. The territorial parish ceased to exist as the states abolished established churches. Once churches were no longer publicly supported the corporation aggregate, the trustee corporation and the corporation sole were developed to permit status to religious societies. In those jurisdictions where no provisions were enacted for corporate existence of religious societies, the leaders of the churches were deemed to be trustees of the ecclesiastical property.

The American law cannot penetrate the religious nature of a purely religious society. First, the American legal system follows the common law doctrine that corporations can be established only by the power of the state.[76] Secondly, the First Amendment to the United States Constitution withdraws from the state any and all capacity for recognizing the Catholic Church or any church in any special mode. Since the state is the sum of political institutions formulated by the body politic to govern the temporal goods of society, the state rests on a purely natural level. As a natural creation, it is unendowed with the supernatural ability to perceive the divine nature of the Church. Other states have in fact placed the Church in a preferred position. This is constitutionally impossible in the United States. One writer, speaking of the nonrecognition stated:

> It is the considered opinion of the writer that the equal status at law position of the Church in America enjoys

---

[75] *Constitution of Virginia*, Art. IV, Sec. 59 and the *Constitution of West Virginia*, Art. VI, Sec. 47, prohibit the forming of religious corporations within their jurisdiction.

[76] *Dartmouth College v. Woodward, N.H.*, 16 U.S. 518, 4 L. Ed. 629.

greater solidarity than it would possess, if it were solely the product of an international convention.[77]

If a religious society does elect to incorporate, the forms of incorporation open to it are: a) the corporation aggregate, b) the trustee corporation and c) the corporation sole. However, no matter what form the religious society adopts the religious corporation remains a private eleemosynary corporation. It does not become a public corporation simply because its status results from a governmental charter. The private nature of the corporate position does not exclude churches from conducting matters of public character. But religious corporations since they are different from public corporations such as the corporation of a town, a city, or a county, come under the prescriptions of private law.[78]

Article 6. Corporation Aggregate

A corporation aggregate is defined as a "juridical person incorporating the members of a parish or congregation."[79] Corporations aggregate are not necessarily similar with reference to their form of management. The incorporation of a parish or of a congregation makes each individual of the parish or the congregation a member of the corporation. Such incorporation of the members transpires despite the fact that only a few persons are specifically mentioned by name in the charter or that the charter extends to many unnamed persons.

When a parish, church or congregation becomes a corporation aggregate, the sovereignty of the legal person is referable to the members themselves, but the exercise of the sovereignty is controlled by the appointment of the corporation's directors. Most statutes of incorporation permit the churches perfect freedom of choice in the selection of the directors that best fits their ecclesiastical nature. So, if the groups thus desire it, all the directors or the greater part of them may consist in ecclesiastical dignitaries.

---

[77] Nessel, *First Amendment Freedoms, Papal Pronouncements and Concordat Practice*, pp. 235-236.

[78] Tyler, *American Ecclesiastical Law* (Albany: N. Y., 1886), p. 105.

[79] Brown, p. 137.

The placement of ecclesiastical officials as members of the corporation's board of directors insures the proper use of the temporalities of the society in accordance with the body's teachings.

A distinctive feature of the so-called New York plan for incorporation of the Roman Catholic societies is that it makes the bishop, the vicar general, and the pastor of each parish *ex officio* to be members of a five man board of directors. The two other board members are laymen selected by the three who *ex officio* are members of the board. The laymen hold office for one year. This one-year appointment allows for an early replacement of a board member should he not have sufficient capabilities or if he fall from union with the Church. The bishop is given the authority as the supervisor of church property within his diocese to declare acts of the corporation board invalid if they have not secured his prior consent. The bishops are likewise empowered by the New York law to divide parishes in accordance with the needs of the Church. The bishop is not responsible in civil law to any other power to exercise this right of division.[80]

Article 7. Trustee Corporation

The trustee corporation is an outgrowth of the former trustee system. When territorial parishes ceased to exist, they were supplanted by voluntary religious societies. These societies were unincorporated. As the societies began to accumulate real property the tenure was placed in a number of trustees chosen by the society to hold the temporalities for the members.[81] The property was in the name of the trustees. This type of possession could give rise to great difficulties. When a trustee died in office, the courts were forced to determine the disposition of the property. The disposition of ecclesiastical property followed from the mode of tenure of the trustee. If the trustee had a life estate, the fee

---

[80] Murphy, *The Laws of the State of New York Affecting Church Property,* The Catholic University of America Canon Law Studies, n. 388 (Washington, D. C.: The Catholic University of America Press, 1957), p. 73.

[81] Zollmann, *American Church Law* (St. Paul: West Publishing Co., 1933), pp. 501-502 (hereafter cited Zollmann).

reverted to the original owner. If the trustee was one of several joint tenants, the fee passed to the surviving trustees. But on the death of the last trustee, the property passed to this trustee's heirs. When the trustee was a tenant in common, his portion ceded immediately to his heirs. Thus, although the members of the congregation had their equity in the property, the legal title could and sometimes did fall into unauthorized hands. The courts of equity could have furnished a remedy, but the churches were not willing to bring the matter to court because of the bitter feelings engendered by such proceedings.

To overcome the liabilities of this form of tenure, the churches petitioned for special charters to permit the incorporation of the trustees.[82] Later these special charters were supplanted by general incorporation statutes. Once the trustees were incorporated the equitable title to the ecclesiastical property vested with the unincorporated societies and the legal title rested in the corporate body rather than in the individual trustees. The death of any one of the trustees did not affect the corporation. Another trustee could be elected or appointed, so that there never was a void in the tenure, and the title was never in abeyance.[83]

The principal difficulty attendant with the trustee corporation rests in the fact that the ecclesiastical body as such lacks all capacity to enter into contractual relations. "The trustees in their corporate capacity have the full control over the civil relations of the Church."[84]

Article 8. Corporation Sole

The

> . . curious phrase "corporation sole" only appears late in the day and seems to be exclusively English but the canonists had come very near to it in their treatment of the cases in which an *ecclesia* had but one cleric con-

[82] *Earle v. Wood,* 62 Mass. 430 (1851).

[83] Zollmann, p. 51.

[84] Bartlett, *The Tenure of Parochial Property in the United States of America,* The Catholic University of America Canon Law Studies, n. 31 (Washington, D. C.. The Catholic University of America, 1926), p. 85.

> nected with it; the *dignitas* or *sedes* or the like could be personified.[85]

A corporation sole consists actually in one person and potentially his successor in some particular office. Through incorporation from the law this person gains certain legal capacities and advantages, in particular that of perpetuity which would be impossible in the natural course of events.

The American practice of corporation sole devolves from English law. In that system, kings, bishops, vicars and others were granted the right to such a form of incorporation to prevent their heirs from obtaining property held by these persons in their official capacities. The nature of the corporation sole was to create a moral personality endowed with a permanent status.

> The present incumbent and his predecessors who lived seven hundred years ago are in law one and the same person, and what was given to the one was given to the others also.[86]

In American civil practice the religious organizations which employ the corporation sole form of tenure enjoy no local sovereignty. The legal and equitable title are vested in the incorporated office.[87] The title vests in the successors in office.

Article 9. Comparison of the Forms of Incorporation

The decree of the Sacred Congregation of the Council[88] has stated that the most preferred form of tenure for the American Church is the form known as the corporation aggregate. This form of incorporation ensures for ecclesiastical property all effective security in civil law while allowing the ordinary to fulfill his civil obligations in accordance with canonical principles. By

---

[85] Pollock-Maitland, *History of English Law* (2 vols., 2 ed., Cambridge. University Press, 1909), I, 502.

[86] Blackstone, I, 469-470.

[87] *Smith v. Bonhovf,* 2 Mich. 115 (1851); *Searle v. Roman Catholic Bishop of Springfield,* 203 Mass. 493, 89 N.E. 809 (1909).

[88] *Supra,* p. 83.

way of majority the members on the board of directors of the corporation are *ex officio* ecclesiastical dignitaries, the bishop, the vicar general, and the pastor in the New York plan. The other two board members are appointed by the ecclesiastical dignitaries. No major act of administration is valid without the consent of the ordinary, and the needed dividing of parishes to assist the faithful in worship is effectively protected.

The corporation aggregate has the further advantage in that the legal title to the ecclesiastical properties rests in the corporate body and the equitable title is in the Church. The corporation inherently enjoys an indefinite term of existence. The change of a bishop or pastor does not affect the civil corporation.

In some states, however, limitations as to sales and mortgages and unjust mortmain statutes as well as accounting requirements make the corporation aggregate unfit for the incorporation of the Roman Catholic Church.[89] Other states, such as New York,[90] Delaware,[91] Minnesota,[92] and Texas[93] have state statutes that permit the corporation aggregate plan of tenure full accordance with the principles of Canon Law. Among the states which effectively secure the rights of the Church the corporation aggregate plan of tenure seems indicated as the best.

In those states which have either no provisions for the incorporation of ecclesiastical societies or which have statutes that are not in best keeping with the provisions of Canon Law, it would seem that the next permissible form of tenure of ecclesiastical

---

[89] Welsh, *The Laws of the State of Nevada Affecting Church Property*, The Catholic University of America Canon Law Studies, n. 409 (Washington, D. C.: The Catholic University of America Press, 1962), pp. 103-109.

[90] Murphy, *The Laws of the State of New York Affecting Church Property*, p. 170.

[91] Schierse, *Laws of the State of Delaware Affecting Church Property*, The Catholic University of America Canon Law Studies, n. 428 (Washington, D. C.: The Catholic University of America Press, 1963), p. 215.

[92] Fleming, *The Laws of the State of Minnesota Affecting Church Property*, The Catholic University of America Canon Law Studies, n. 438 (Washington, D. C.: microfilm, 1964), p. 186.

[93] McLeaish, *The Laws of Texas Affecting Church Property*, The Catholic University of America Canon Law Studies, n. 405 (Washington, D. C.: The Catholic University of America Press, 1960), p. 187.

temporalities would be the holding of the property in the form of the corporation sole. The corporation does permit the ordinary to hold the property in a civilly recognized manner that reflects the desires of Rome. The ordinary has, apart from his natural life, a civil existence that permits the orderly transfer of property to his successors. In the supervision of the goods of the corporation, the ordinary is free to apply the rules of the universal laws of the Church.

The corporation sole method of tenure begets two limitations. It is a matter of conjecture how a state statute would be construed with reference to the nature of tenure by the sole corporator. Secondly, the absence of a statute so detailing the interim period of the vacancy of the incorporator's office produces an abeyance of the fee, so that no one is duly qualified civilly to transact business during this period.[94] Difficulties incidental to the interim period can be precluded by means of a statutory amendment, as was enacted by the District of Columbia.[95]

Nevertheless, a corporation sole system, since it vests the powers of acquisition, tenure, and administration of ecclesiastical goods in one person, is in opposition to the provisions of the Code of Canon Law. The Code declares that all ecclesiastical property is owned by the ecclesiastical moral personality.[96] This is not true in the corporation sole mode of tenure; in the corporation sole tenure of property the title is vested in a physical person. Again, Canon Law envisions a form of tenure wherein each parish, as a moral personality, will own the property of that entity. In the corporation sole manner of tenure the ordinary is the administrator of all ecclesiastical goods of the incorporated diocese. The Code of Canon Law declares that the ordinary is the supervisor not the administrator of the goods of the diocese. The pastor is the ordinary administrator. The bishop is vested with the duty of supervising the proper execution of the pastor's official duties.[97] The local bishop is directed to have a board of administrators chosen

---

[94] Rodriquez, pp. 134-138.

[95] Chapter 355, 2nd Session, 80th Congress, Act of 29 May 1948 (HR 6203).

[96] *CIC.*, can. 1499, § 2.

[97] *CIC.*, can. 1519, § 1.

because of their competence in civil law to assist him in judging which form of incorporation is best suited for the needs of his own territory.

The trust system of tenure is deemed the best form in Mississippi[98] and in Ohio.[99] In Ohio charitable and benevolent institutions under the ownership, control and management of religious communities belonging to the Catholic Church are separately incorporated as a corporation aggregate.[100] When a bishop of a diocese holds the parochial property in trust, the arrangements may be said to have most of the advantages of the system of absolute ownership without its dangers. The bishop has the legal title to the property, and as the legal owner he can administer the property in accordance with the provisions of the universal law. He can place the goods of the diocese in the hands of a board of administrators while retaining the right to remove them if this be the wiser course. He can always supervise the administration of the property in accordance with Canon Law while not endangering the property of the Church. In the event that the bishop suffers any financial losses, the losses can not be attached to the ecclesiastical goods in his care.[101] Even if he died without a will, the property remains with the *cestui que* trust as its equitable owner.

Trust tenure somewhat approximates the tenure of property as specified in Canon Law. The pastor when duly appointed to a parish acquires the right of administering the property, which right accrues to him by civil law also. The equitable title remains with the parish as the *cestui que* trust, and this reflects the idea that the ecclesiastical moral personality is the proper owner of the goods. In the separation of legal title and equitable title in American civil law there is the implicit recognition of the proper ownership as vested in the ecclesiastical moral personality. The system of tenure through a trusteeship practically gives the Church rights under the civil law which it would not otherwise be capable

[98] McGough, p. 192.
[99] Wiggins, p. 128.
[100] Wiggins, p. 75.
[101] *Mannix v. Purcell*, 26 Ohio 102.

of possessing, since the civil law withholds all formal recognition of the ecclesiastical moral personality.

The system of trust tenure has one inherent problem. The civil courts have an absolute control over all trusts, and therefore they have control over ecclesiastical properties held in trust.[102] Thus, the bishop has been declared by some judiciaries as a mere depository of the legal property. In one case, the courts were not empowered to convey the parochial property to the bishop after the property had been purchased with parochial funds by the priest assigned there due to a doubtful trust instrument.[103]

The courts have stated that the trust gives rise to a certain amount of confusion as to how a court will determine the trust instrument. Moreover, the tenure of property under a trustee does not conform to the prescriptions of canon law. The ordinary administrator of ecclesiastical property is the pastor, not the bishop. The bishop has the right to enact standards of management for the pastors to follow, but the bishop remains in the Church's universal law merely the supervisor of such properties, not the administrator.

In summation, the best form of tenure appears to be the corporation aggregate form of tenure. The next best would seem to be the corporation sole, while the trustee corporation and the trustee tenure as such are liable to court interpretations of the instrument of the trusts which have been charged to their care.

SECTION 3. APPENDIX

Article 1. Formal Relations Between the United States and the Papal States

It is interesting to note that the United Stats had diplomatic relations at one time with the Papal States. The election of Pope Pius IX generated considerable attention in the United States, and there was widespread action to establish diplomatic relations with the Papal States.

> The reforms instituted by Pius IX called forth generous expressions of satisfaction from his subjects, and attracted

[102] Zollmann, pp. 357-361.

[103] *Saint Patrick's Catholic Church v. Daly*, 116 Ill. 76, 4 N.E. 241 (1886).

> the attention, not only of other states in Italy, but of the countries of the civilized world. Sentiment in the United States was in accord with that expression in Italy.[104]

The United States public press supported diplomatic relations with the Papal States. In his State of the Union Address President James Polk (1795-1849) in line with that public opinion included a recommendation for the opening of diplomatic relations in these words:

> The Secretary of State has submitted an estimate to defray the expenses of opening diplomatic relations with the Papal States. The interesting political events now in progress in these States, as well as a just regard to our commercial interest have in my opinion rendered such a measure highly expedient.[105]

There was a violent disagreement in Congress concerning the presidential recommendation. After debate, the House of Representatives passed the measure 137 to 15 and the Senate confirmed the action 36-7. The first appropriation was for a chargé d'affaires. A minister resident was later assigned to Rome.

> The United States mission to the Papal States was the rare, probably unique instance of diplomatic relations with the Pope purely in his capacity of temporal sovereign. . . . The debates that took place in both the House and the Senate reflect agreement that while the Pope enjoyed a double character—that of religious chief and political sovereign—the United States mission necessarily would deal with the Pope solely in his latter capacity.[106]

In 1867, the mission to the Papal States was terminated be-

---

[104] Feiertag, *American Public Opinion on the Diplomatic Relations between the United States and the Papal States (1847-1867)*. A dissertation of the Graduate School of Arts and Science of the Catholic University of America (Washington: The Catholic University of America, 1933), p. 5.

[105] *Congressional Globe,* 30th Congress, 1st Session, 1847-48, p. 8.

[106] Graham, *Vatican Diplomacy, A Study of Church and State on the International Plane* (Princeton, N. J.: Princeton University Press, 1959), p. 83.

cause Congress refused to continue the necessary financial appropriations.

Article 2. Recognition of Moral Personalities Created by the Church

There were no formal relations between the United States and the Papal States after the termination of Congressional appropriations until the Treaty of Paris was concluded ending the Spanish American War. The United States acquired properties from the Spanish Crown through this instrument. Part of the land so acquired included property owned by the Holy See and the Catholic Dioceses established in the Philippines and in Puerto Rico. The United States Supreme Court in two of its decisions[107] acknowledged that the rights in property and the public moral personalities established by the Church were recognized by the United States of America in accordance with the principles of international law.

Article 3. Personal Representation at the Vatican

During the Second World War, the President of the United States sent Myron Taylor (1874-1959) as his personal representative to the Vatican. In the United States, there was a clear acceptation that this representative of the President was merely a personal liaison between the President and the Vatican. However, the same conditional recognition of the representative of Mr. Roosevelt (1882-1945) was not so received in Europe. Mr. Taylor was listed among the Vatican diplomatic corps and was at all the public meetings of the Pontiff with the members of the diplomatic corps.

President Truman attempted to re-institute formal relations between the United States and the Vatican in the latter part of the 1940's. He nominated General Mark Clark, the former military

---

[107] *Municipality of Ponce v. Roman Catholic Apostolic Church in Puerto Rico,* 210 U.S. 296, 28 S. Ct. 737, 52 L. Ed. 1068 (1908); *Santos v. Holy Roman Catholic and Apostolic Church, Philippine,* 212 U.S. 463, 29 S. Ct. 338, 53 L. Ed. 599 (1908).

commander in Italy to serve in the post. However, the Senate allowed neither the appointment nor the institution of diplomatic relations with the Holy See.

Article 4. The Holy See and the United Nations

The United States is in informal communication with the Holy See through the various agencies of the United Nations. The Holy See is an accredited observer to this world body. Together with the United States, the Holy See is a member of the Universal Postal Union and the International Union for Telecommunications. The Holy See is a permanent observer to two other committees of the United Nations: a) United Nations Education, Scientific and Cultural Organization located in Paris and b) the Food and Agricultural Organization located in Rome. The Holy See is a member of the Consultative Committee for the High Commissioner for Refugees which is located in Geneva. It also participates in meetings called by various United Nations committees without being a member or having an official observer to the committees. The Holy See is also a founding member of the International Atomic Energy Agency which is closely related to the United Nations. Through all these committees the Holy See and the United States enter into informal communication.

In October, 1965, the Holy Father, Pope Paul VI, formally addressed the United Nations on the subject of world peace. He was received by that body as the spiritual head of a religious group. While in New York, the Pontiff met informally with President Lyndon B. Johnson and discussed problems of mutual interest with the President.

CHAPTER V

Some Particular Questions in Church and State Relations

SECTION 1. INTEGRITY OF MEETINGS

In the previous chapter the right of any religious society to exist was discussed. It was there noted that the Supreme Court ruled that "The right to organize voluntary religious associations to assist in the expression and dissemination of any religious doctrine . . . is unquestioned."[1] This ruling flows from the rights of citizens under the First Amendment of the Constitution.

To have an effective right to enter into religious associations, the citizens in their act of worship must be guaranteed the right of peaceful assembly. Civil protection of the religious meetings begins when the communicants first assemble prior to the service. The civil authorities will ensure the protection of the religious adherents during the meeting and through their dispersal. Individuals

> . . have the right to convene on church grounds for that purpose [worship], to enter the church, and engage in religious worship, and, after church, to disperse without being disturbed, made afraid, or annoyed by profanity, fighting on the part of any persons, who by their conduct wilfully and maliciously interrupt or disturb the congregation assembled for religious worship. . . . The congregation has the right to convene, worship, and disperse without malicious or wilful interruption. . . [2]

The courts have prosecuted the persons attempting to interrupt the orderly acts of religious worship.[3] In addition to excluding

---

[1] *Watson v. Jones,* 80 U.S. 679, 20 L. Ed. 666.

[2] *State v. Matheny,* 122 S. C. 459, 101 S.E. 666 (1919); *Richardson v. State,* 5 Tex. App. 470 (1880).

[3] *Ellis v. State,* 10 Ala. App. 252, 65 So. 412 (1914): *Kinney v. State,* 38 Ala. 224 (1862); *Love v. State,* 35 Tex. Crim. 27, 29 S.W. 790 (1895); *State v. Wright,* 41 Ark. 410, 48 Am. Rep. 43 (1883).

persons who come from the outside to disturb the religious meetings, the courts will vindicate the right of the religious organization to expel members from the religious group and prevent their attendance at religious exercises.[4]

SECTION 2. THE RIGHT OF THE CHURCH TO TEACH

Article 1. The Right of the Church to Pronounce Its Doctrine

The immediate task of the Roman Catholic Church is to proclaim the faith of Christ. Our Lord commissioned the Apostles to ". . go into the whole world and preach the gospel to every creature."[5] The Code of Canon Law states:

> Christ Our Lord confided to the Church the deposit of faith, in order that she with the perpetual assistance of the Holy Ghost, might faithfully preserve and expound the revealed doctrine. Independently of any civil power whatsoever, the Church has the right and duty to teach all nations the evangelical doctrine, and all are bound by the divine law to acquire a proper knowledge of this doctrine and to embrace the true Church of God.[6]

The principal task of proclaiming the gospel of Christ is confided to the Pope as the Vicar of Christ on Earth and to the bishops. The Pope is endowed with the prerogative of infallibility when *ex cathedra,* in the matters of faith and morals, he teaches the faithful.[7] The bishops have an equal duty in union with the Pope to proclaim to their flocks the teachings of the faith.[8]

The right of the Church to profess its doctrine and bring it to all the citizens of the United States is guaranteed by the First

---

[4] *Carter v. Papineau,* 222 Mass. 464, 111 N.E. 358 (1916); *Fitzgerald v. Robinson,* 112 Mass. 371 (1873).

[5] *Mark,* 16: 15.

[6] *CIC.,* can. 1322.

[7] *CIC.,* can. 1323.

[8] *De Ecclesia,* n. 25: "For the bishops are preachers of the faith, who lead new disciples to Christ, and they are authentic teachers endowed with the authority of Christ, who preach to the people committed to them the faith they must believe and put into practice, and by the light of Holy Spirit, illustrate the faith."

Amendment of the Federal Constitution. The Supreme Court in *Watson v. Jones*[9] declared:

> In this country the full and free right to entertain any religious belief, to practice any religious principle, and to teach any religious doctrine which does not violate the laws of morality and property, and which does not infringe personal rights, is conceded to all.

The courts will not tolerate any attempts to place governmental institutions in the position of dictating religious opinions or doctrines. In *West Virginia State Board of Education v. Barnett*[10] the Supreme Court stated:

> If there is any fixed star in our constitution it is that no official, high or petty, can prescribe what shall be orthodox in politics, nationalism, religion, or other matters of opinion or force citizens to confess by word or act faith therein.

The public policy of the United States permits no intrusion into the citizen's freedom of religious expression. This policy is evidenced in the suit of *United States v. Ballard*.[11]

The case arose from the government contention that the accused used religion as a tool to cloak their fraudulently conducted practices. Guy W. Ballard, Edna W. Ballard and Donald Ballard were brought to trial as organizers of the religious movement known as the "I Am" Movement. The indictment charged the defendants had fraudulently represented Guy W. Ballard alias St. Germain, Jesus, George Washington as a specially selected divine messenger. In reversing the lower court, the Supreme Court ruled:

> . . . the Circuit Court of Appeals held that the question of truth of the representations concerning the respondent's religious doctrines or beliefs should be submitted to the jury. . . . Whatever this particular indictment

[9] *Watson v. Jones*, 80 U.S. 679, 20 L. Ed. 666.

[10] *West Virginia State Board of Education v. Barnett*, 319 U.S. 624, 68 S. Ct. 1178, 87 L. Ed. 1628 (1943).

[11] *United States v. Ballard*, 322 U.S. 78, 64 S. Ct. 882, 88 L. Ed. 1148 (1944).

> might require, the First Amendment precludes such a course. . . . Freedom of thought, which includes religious beliefs, is basic in a society of free men. It embraces the right to maintain theories of life and death and of the hereafter which are rank heresies to the followers of the orthodox faiths. Heresy trials are foreign to our Constitution. Men may believe what they cannot prove. They may not be put to the proof of their religious doctrines or beliefs. . . . The religious views espoused by the respondents might seem incredible, if not preposterous, to most people. But if these doctrines are subject to trial before a jury charged with finding their truth or falsity, then the same can be done with the religious beliefs of any sect. When the triers of fact undertake that task, they enter forbidden domain.[12]

Religious beliefs are so fundamental to the American system of democracy that no legislature or judicatory agency of either the federal or the state governments may infringe or attempt to judge these liberties. The people did not give such power to the federal government and it may not use any power with which it is not endowed.

> The First Amendment to the Constitution, in declaring that Congress shall make no law respecting the establishment of religion or forbidding the free exercise thereof, was intended to allow everyone under the jurisdiction of the United States to entertain such notions respecting his relations to his Maker and the duties they impose as may be approved by his judgment, and conscience, and to exhibit his sentiments in such form or worship as he may think proper, not injurious to the equal rights of others, and to prohibit legislation for the support of any religious tenets, or modes of worship of any sect.[13]

Article 2. Proselytizing

a) Definition

Proselytizing is the effort that is made to induce persons to join one particular faith when they have either had no religious affilia-

[12] *Loc. cit.*

[13] *Davis v. Beason,* 133 U.S. 333, 10 S. Ct. 299, 33 L. Ed. 637 (1890).

tion or have had a prior religious membership. The forms of proselytizing include personal contact, distribution of literature, house to house visitation, and preaching in public places. The freedom of proselytizing flows not only from the religious guarantees of the First Amendment but also from the independent guarantees of freedom of speech, press and assembly. The freedom of press guarantees the right of distributing religious material, while the professed street corner preacher is protected by the right of free speech and assembly.

b) Prior Restrictions

Government is forbidden to enact statutes that place prior restrictions on the dissemination of religious doctrines. The effect of placing prior restrictions on the freedom of religious expression has the nature of censorship, the central evil against which the First Amendment is directed.[14]

Laws relating to the right of an individual to spread his religious beliefs developed as a result of attempts by local and state governments to prohibit or regulate forms of proselytizing that affect the community as a whole and conflict with some community interest. The government has the preservation of peace and order as its primary concern. This duty has precedence over the right of an individual to speak his mind. Should the two conflict, the state may invoke penal sanctions against such an individual when his words tend to incite his listeners to riot, disorder or other examples of unlawful conduct. Hence advocates of a religious belief may not use what are termed "fighting" words in a religious gathering. A statute prohibiting such verbalizations even during the course of a religious gathering is constitutional.[15]

But a person may not be punished civilly for the simple reason that his views can be construed as an offense to the religious sensitivities of his auditors. Indeed, part of the right of freedom of speech is the right to criticize the views held by others. Such

---

[14] *Thomas v. Collins*, 323 U.S. 516, 65 S. Ct. 315, 89 L. Ed. 430 (1945).

[15] *Chaplinsky v. New Hampshire*, 315 U.S. 568, 62 S. Ct. 766, 86 L. Ed. 1031 (1942).

an attack may not in itself be punished as an incitement to a breach of the peace,[16] even if a public disturbance in fact occurs.[17] The law enforcement agencies have the grave obligation of protecting a citizen's right to public speech. However when the police force is inadequate to defend the speaker of unpopular views, or when riotous reaction appears certain, the police may request the orator to curtail his talk and arrest him if he does not comply with the police.[18]

The Supreme Court has maintained that the police may not prohibit the speaker in advance when it is feared that some disturbance will occur as a consequence of the talk.[19] In addition, the courts will strike down as invalid vaguely drawn state statutes when these enactments, in forbidding all loitering or breach of the peace, nevertheless, because of their general tone discourage by fear of arrest the lawful expression of free speech, which stands guaranteed by constitutional right.[20]

c) The Use of Public Streets and Parks

The use of the streets and parks of a town often brings forth a conflict between the personal guarantees of religious freedom and the legitimate exercise of the police power. The obligation of maintaining peace and order has been at times a barrier to religious parades and street-corner preaching. The Supreme Court has maintained that the application of civil restrictions to the dissemination of commercial leaflets does not apply to the distribution of religious leaflets on public highways.[21] The Supreme Court has similarly ruled that there is a constitutional right to speak and assemble in public parks and on public streets.[22]

---

[16] *Cantwell v. Connecticut,* 310 U.S. 296, 60 S. Ct. 980, 84 L. Ed. 1213.

[17] *Terminiello v. City of Chicago,* 337 U.S. 1, 69 S. Ct. 894, 93 L. Ed. 1311 (1949).

[18] *Feiner v. New York,* 340 U.S. 315, 71 S. Ct. 303, 95 L. Ed. 295 (1951).

[19] *Kunz v. New York,* 340 U.S. 290, 71 S. Ct. 312, 95 L. Ed. 280 (1951).

[20] *Cantwell v. Connecticut,* 310 U.S. 296, 60 S. Ct. 980, 84 L. Ed. 1213; *Thornhill v. Alabama,* 310 U.S. 88, 60 S. Ct. 736, 84 L. Ed. 1093 (1940).

[21] *Murdock v. Pennsylvania,* 319 U.S. 105, 63 S. Ct. 891, 87 L. Ed. 1292 (1943); *Schneider v. State,* 308 U.S. 147, 60 S. Ct. 146, 84 L. Ed. 155 (1939).

[22] *Hague v. CIO,* 307 U.S. 496, 59 S. Ct. 954, 83 L. Ed. 1423 (1939).

Correlatively the civil authorities may require a license for parades and processions in order to protect the public convenience in the use of streets. However, in such instances the licensing authority must not be vested with an arbitrary and dictatorial power.[23] The Court has held such licensing reasonable because of the increased expense of policing such functions and of protecting the constitutional rights of the citizens during their public expression of worship. The state has a similar competence for regulating the use of sound equipment.[24] The town or municipality may probably reserve some of its parks as places for family recreation, and thus may prohibit public addresses and mass meetings therein. However, it would appear extremely doubtful if the town could so reserve all of its recreational areas.

d) House to House Solicitation

Proselytizers seeking converts and contributions by way of house to house visitations do not have a constitutional right to enter private property once they have been informed that they are not welcome. Thus, owners of private apartment buildings, hotels, and parks may lawfully exclude such operations on their premises.[25] In contradistinction, solicitation may not be prohibited upon private property when such property has the nature of public property from its long usage, as in the case of a company owned town[26] or a governmentally owned town.[27] Hence, if the owner of property has held the property open to the public universally, the owner may not arbitrarily restrict the constitutional rights of members entering his property.

There can be no doubt that a town or city has as its primary purpose the preservation of the public order within the community. However unpopular may appear certain advocates of religious

---

[23] *Cox v. New Hampshire,* 312 U.S. 569, 61 S. Ct. 762, 85 L. Ed. 1049 (1941).

[24] *Kovacs v. Cooper,* 336 U.S. 77, 69 S. Ct. 448, 93 L. Ed. 513 (1949).

[25] *Watchtower Bible & Tract Society v. Metropolitan Life Insurance Company,* 297 N.Y. 339, 79 N.E. 2d 433 (1948); cert. denied, 335 U.S. 886, 69 S. Ct. 432, 93 L. Ed. 425 (1948).

[26] *Marsh v. Alabama,* 326 U.S. 501, 66 S. Ct. 276, 90 L. Ed. 265 (1946).

[27] *Tucker v. Texas,* 326 U.S. 517, 66 S. Ct. 274, 90 L. Ed. 274 (1945).

doctrine, or however persistent they may appear in their diligence, these persons may not be prohibited from distributing religious leaflets or doctrines in a door to door manner. The distribution of religious literature from house to house has been held to be a religious practice secured by the First Amendment. It is on the same high plane as other forms of worship.[28] Towns may not therefore prohibit such activities generally or specifically. The objection that the adherents are in fact selling religious material does not place such persons so engaged within purview of commercial restrictions. Since such an activity has a religious purpose, the endeavor warrants a higher form of protection.[29]

Towns however may seek to protect their citizens by requiring a prior registration of house to house proselytizers. To sustain such a registration the towns may constitutionally impose a modest fee to defray the costs of the registration systems.[30] In the use of such a registration system the decision in the *Cantwell v. Connecticut* case must always be observed, i.e., the public official may not be so empowered as to prohibit arbitrarily through such registrations the right to seek converts or the dissemination of one's religious views.[31]

e) Taxation of Proselytizing Activities

States and towns are prohibited from placing a tax or licensing fee upon the proselytizing activities as such. It has been noted that a modest fee may be enacted to cover the increased costs of police protections at parades, and fees may be imposed to cover the registration of proselytizers. However, it is forbidden to place a tax on the distribution of religious printed matter or to tax preachers as such. In *Murdock v. Pennsylvania*[32] the City of Jeanette enacted an ordinance demanding such a license fee of all canvassers or solicitors. The Jehovah Witnesses failed to

---

[28] *Murdock v. Pennsylvania,* 319 U.S. 105, 63 S. Ct. 891, 87 L. Ed. 1292.

[29] *Jamison v. State of Texas,* 318 U.S. 415, 63 S. Ct. 669, 87 L. Ed. 869 (1943).

[30] *Murdock v. Pennsylvania,* 319 U.S. 105, 63 S. Ct. 891, 87 L. Ed. 1292.

[31] *Cantwell v. Connecticut,* 310 U.S. 296, 60 S. Ct. 980, 84 L. Ed. 1213.

[32] *Murdock v. Pennsylvania,* 319 U.S. 105, 63 S. Ct. 891, 87 L. Ed. 1292.

comply with the statute and were convicted of violating this ordinance. On appeal to the Supreme Court, the Court struck down the tax, since a tax laid on a freedom guaranteed by the First Amendment was unconstitutional. The Court equated such a tax to a tool of censorship.

> The power to impose a license tax on the exercise of these freedoms [of the First Amendment] is indeed as potent as the power of censorship which this Court has repeatedly struck down.[33]

Property owned by the religious groups can be taxed as well as the incomes of persons engaged in religious callings. But the act of spreading the faith of a citizen may not be taxed, since his freedom of belief and his right to persuade others of the validity of his religious tenets are guaranteed by the First Amendment.

f) Parents Using Their Children to Proselytize

A parent is not excused from regulations protecting the activities of minors, even when the child is engaged in proselytizing. A mother's conviction was sustained by the Supreme Court after she was found guilty of having her child distribute religious literature at a late hour of the evening. The mother argued that the statute regulating the child's activities with reference to the hour of the day was an unconstitutional invasion of religious liberty. The court sustained the conviction and contended that the state can exercise authority in respect to the child over and above parental responsibility.

> We think with reference to the public proclaiming of religion, upon the streets and in other public places, the power of the state to control the conduct of children reaches beyond the scope of its authority over adults, as is true in the case of other freedoms, and the rightful boundary of its power has not been crossed in this case.[34]

The preceding pages offered an analysis of the rights and the

---

[33] *Loc. cit.*

[34] *Prince v. Massachusetts,* 321 U.S. 158, 64 S. Ct. 438, 88 L. Ed. 645 (1945).

limitations placed on the state and federal government with reference to religious beliefs and the spread of religious doctrines. It has been noted that the religious freedoms have been placed "in a preferred position."[35] The Constitution will permit no governmental agency to examine the claims of a religious doctrine, nor will the Constitution allow any curb to be enacted in reference to the free dissemination of religious teachings.

The Roman Catholic Church participates in these freedoms, as do all the other religious groups within the United States. The Church is guaranteed the right to teach and fulfill its commission. Although the divine foundation of the Church cannot be recognized constitutionally, nevertheless the Church can fulfill its task independently of governmental control. This independent freedom vindicated supernaturally for the Church by Christ is guaranteed naturally under the Constitution of the United States. Not only does the Constitution guarantee the Church's rights, but the full weight of civil power has been and will be exercised should any agency attempt to limit the Church's freedom and right to bring the message of Christ to all men.

SECTION 3. THE RIGHT OF THE CHURCH TO MAINTAIN SCHOOLS

The Church has been entrusted with the solemn duty of preaching the word of God to all men. One ordinary means that the Church employs to discharge its teaching commission is to erect its own schools and to govern these institutions.[36] This educational right of the Church is proper to itself and native. The Church by its divine institution is the religious teacher of men.[37] Inasmuch as the Church brings men into the order of grace through baptism and nourishes them with the sacraments, the Church must have the right to cultivate the entire man, and to enrich his faculties, natural and supernatural, in leading him to his final

---

[35] *Murdock v. Pennsylvania,* 319 U.S. 105, 63 S. Ct. 891, 87 L. Ed. 1292.

[36] De Pauw, *The Legal Status of Catholic Elementary Schools in Belgium, 1830-1950,* The Catholic University of America Canon Law Studies, n. 336 (Washington, D. C.: The Catholic University of America Press, 1953), p. 17.

[37] Matthew, 28: 18-20.

and eternal destiny. Over and above the supernatural office of the Church, the Church would have the right to schools from the merely natural law. The natural law concedes to all competent associations the right to found and conduct schools. Should one deny the supernatural character of the Church such a person would have to admit that at least the Church cannot be denied the right to its own schools guaranteed to all natural associations. The Church under the natural law itself, has the right to conduct schools. The natural law concedes to all competent associations the right to found and conduct schools. This right cannot therefore be denied to the Church, since it is a juridic person possessed of the most outstanding advantages for establishing and successfully governing schools.

While the right of the Church to establish and conduct schools is proper and native to itself, it is nevertheless indirect. The right to conduct schools is warranted not for the exclusively direct attainment of its end and for the exclusively direct fulfillment of its teaching office, but for the inclusively indirect implementation of its teaching office.

The Church's right to establish schools is partial and cumulative, i.e., it is not exclusive. The Church is not the only society entrusted with the task of education. The family and the state have a proper concern in the educational process. The state has the right to protect itself and its subjects from harm by insisting that the children be given an adequate education. Pius XI taught the state has a true and just right in education, which flows from its nature as a society founded with divine sanction.[38] It must always be noted that the parent is the primary and principal authority entrusted with the responsibility for the education of children.[39]

The right of the Church to conduct its own schools is furthermore independent of any human authority. It pertains to the Church as a juridically perfect society to conduct its schools without having this right conferred on itself by any civil agency.

---

[38] Pius XI, Encyclical, *Divini illius Magistri,* 31 dec. 1929—*AAS*, XXLL (1930), 62.

[39] *Summa Theologica,* IIa, IIae. q. 10 a. 12.

The Catholic Church declares that it alone has the right to establish Catholic Universities and faculties. The founding of such faculties and universities is reserved exclusively to the Apostolic See.[40] Here the expression of the law is not as generic and sweeping as it first appears. The Holy See reserves to itself the right to establish those universities which confer an ecclesiastical degree, i.e., one in Theology, in Scripture, in Canon Law or in Philosophy.[41] The Code speaks of two things, a Catholic University and a Catholic faculty. Some state universities in Europe have a Catholic faculty for theology by agreement between the Church and the State. In the United States there is one professed Catholic University in the full sense of Canon Law. It is the Catholic University of America, established in Washington, D. C., with the right of conferring all the above listed ecclesiastical degrees. The Holy See does not desire at present to confer the title and the faculties of an Ecclesiastical University on any other Catholic school in the United States.[42]

There are in the United States other Catholic colleges and universities. These are ecclesiastical moral personalities established in accordance with the rules for non-collegiate moral persons at the discretion of the local bishop.[43]

The local ordinary has the right to establish within his jurisdiction schools of every grade for the instruction of the children of the Church. The Third Plenary Council of Baltimore (1884) directed each parish to establish an elementary school. The bishops were charged with the duty to see there was a full compliance with this injunction, and Pastors who refused to heed this prescription, when it was possible for them to do so, were to be removed from office.[44] The educational laws of the Third Council

---

[40] *CIC.*, can. 1376.

[41] *CIC.*, can. 1377.

[42] Woywod, Smith, *A Practical Commentary on the Code of Canon Law* (2 vols. in 1, revised ed., New York: Joseph F. Wagner, Inc., 1957), II, 138.

[43] *CIC.*, can. 1489.

[44] *Acta et Decreta Concilii Plenarii Baltimorensis Tertii, 1884* (Baltimore: John Murphy and Co., 1886): Titulus VI—*De Iuventutis Institutione,* n. 199: "Quibus omnibus bene perpensis statuimus et decernimus: 1. Prope unamquamque ecclesiam ubi nondum existit, scholam parochialem intra duos

of Baltimore are still in force in the United States.[45] However it must be noted that, when a parish cannot afford to establish an elementary school, the law does not bind until such times as funds are available.

The supervision of the schools within a diocese falls to the local ordinary. He has the right and duty to watch over any school within his territory, to see that nothing offensive to faith and morals is offered to the students.[46] Fundamentally (*per se*) the bishop's duty of vigilance extends to all the schools which are in his territory, be they private or public, when they are attended by Catholic students.[47] In the educational system of the United States wherein the boards of education are not permitted to include religious training in public school curriculums this duty of the local ordinary is indeed lessened.

The ordinary's duty to be vigilant over the religious and moral instructions given the students in Catholic institutions confers upon him the right of visitation in all such educational institutions within the diocese, even those of exempt religious, unless there be question of purely internal community schools, which serve for the professed of an exempt religious institute.[48]

Catholics are required by church law to attend institutions under the Church's vigilance.[49] This prescription flows from the im-

---

annos a promulgatione huius Concilii erigendam et in perpetuum sustentandam esse, nisi Episcopus ob graviores difficultates dilationem concedendum esse judicet. 2. Sacerdotem, qui intra hoc tempus erectionem vel sustentationem scholae gravi sua negligentia impediat, vel post repetitas Episcopi admonitiones non curet, mereri remotionem ab illa ecclesia."

[45] Cf. *CIC.*, can. 6.

[46] *CIC.*, can. 1381, § 2.

[47] Pope Pius XI, Encyclical *Divini Illius Magistri,* the Christian Education of Youth, 31 December, 1929, *AAS,* XXLL (1930), 49-97. Translation from the American Press, New York, 1936, p. 7: "Again it is the inalienable right, as well as the indispensable duty of the Church, to watch over the entire education of her children, in all institutions, public or private, not merely in regard to the religious instruction there given, but in regard to every other branch of learning and every regulation insofar as religion and morality are concerned."

[48] *CIC.*, can. 1382.

[49] *CIC.*, can. 1374.

portance of inculcating religious doctrines in every age of scholarship. With growth in his secular learning the student should grow also in the knowledge of God. The learning process is not limited to merely elementary or secondary scholarship. When Catholic institutions are physically or morally not available to the student, the scholar may attend the neutral, mixed or non-Catholic institution with the permission of the local ordinary.[50]

The courts of the nation have recognized the independent right to establish schools other than public schools. The existence of private schools was accorded a final sanction once for all in *Pierce v. Society of Sisters.*[51] In its ruling the Court declared that the primary responsibility of education is vested not in the state but in the parents.

> The fundamental theory of liberty upon which all governments of this Union repose excludes any general power of the State to standardize its children by forcing them to accept instruction from public teachers only. The child is not the mere creature of the State: those who nurture him and direct his destiny have the right, coupled with the high duty, to recognize and prepare him for additional obligations.[52]

The decision of the Court reflects the attitude that there are more than merely civil obligations incumbent on the members of society. The parents have a proper right to select those institutions of learning for their own children. Men must have a proper knowledge of all his responsibilities and duties to God, to society, and to his family if he is adequately to progress toward maturity. The development of his religious convictions is a proper concern necessitating attendance at religiously oriented schools.

The institutions selected by the parents to inculcate the additional duties spoken of in the Court decision have a right to exist. As a corporation, such institutions have valid property interests and rights protected by the due process clause of the Fourteenth Amendment. Injunctions against an arbitrary action of any govern-

---

[50] *CIC.,* can. 1375.

[51] *Pierce v. Society of Sisters,* 268 U.S. 510, 45 S. Ct. 571, 69 L. Ed. 1070 (1925).

[52] *Loc. cit.*

mental agency to deprive these institutions of their rights are clearly in opposition to the *Pierce* ruling.

The *Pierce* ruling demands that no school can be closed simply because it is a religious school under the direction of the Church. The closing under these reasons would be an unwarranted intrusion of property interests. However, the State does have a valid interest in the educational development of its citizens.

> The object of our school laws is not only to protect the state from the consequences of ignorance, but also to guard against the dangers of incompetent citizenship.[53]

The various states have the right to compel attendance at organized classes. In *Pierce v. Society of Sisters* the Court took note that this right of compulsory attendance is a true prerogative of the states. They have the right

> . . reasonably to regulate all schools, to inspect, supervise and examine them, their teachers, and pupils. [54]

The state must conduct the supervision. However, parents may not offer such educational facilities to the students which would demand that the state expend an unreasonable amount of time and money to conduct the examinations.

> If the parent undertakes to make use of units so small, or facilities of doubtful quality, that supervision thereof would impose an unreasonable burden on the state, he offends against the reasonable provisions for schools which can be supervised without unreasonable expense.[55]

Various jurisdictions permit home study courses to satisfy the law of compulsory attendance,[56] while others clearly forbid such practices.[57] But whether or not the jurisdictions accept or reject home study practices, the states do maintain as their right the

[53] *New Hampshire v. Hoyt,* 84 N.H. 38, 146 Atl. 170 (1929).

[54] *Pierce v. Society of Sisters,* 268 U.S. 510, 45 S. Ct. 571, 69 L. Ed. 1070.

[55] *New Hampshire v. Hoyt,* 84 N.H. 38, 146 Atl. 170.

[56] *People of Illinois v. Levinsen,* 404 Ill. 574, 90 N.E. 2d. 213 (1950); *State v. Peterman,* 32 Ind. App. 665, 70 N.E. 550 (1904).

[57] *Stephens v. Bongart,* 15 N.J. Misc. 80, 189 Atl. 131 (1937); *State v. Will,* 99 Kan. 167, 160 P. 1025 (1916); *State v. Pilkington,* 310 S.W. 2d. 304 (1958); *Rice v. Commonwealth,* 188 Va. 224, 49 S.E. 2d. 342 (1948).

prerogative of establishing minimum standards for the instructions of students. Such a prerogative includes both the supervision of the qualifications for teachers and the courses given.

The state has a valid concern in the education of its citizens. It must provide for the general education of all its members. The educational function of the state is designed to assist the parents who have the primary responsibility of providing education for their children. In co-operating and working with the parents the state should be able to list the minimal skills for its territory in arranging the courses of instruction. In supervising the quality of education in public and private institutions of learning the state is well within its proper field of endeavor. The state in so acting does not infringe on the Church's right to maintain its own schools. The Code of Canon Law does not necessarily exclude or forbid the visiting of its schools by state agencies. The universal law of the Church does not state that the Church's educational rights are in all matters independent of civil authority.[58]

It must be pointed out in this context that the supervision of religious educational standards are the sole responsibility of the Church alone.[59] Any interference with the religious instructions are a clear violation of church law. In fact, the Constitution of the United States prohibits any attempt of any civil official to regulate matters of religious orthodoxy.[60]

Religious principles do not give rise to a valid objection to compulsory school attendance statutes. In one case a Moslem boy absented himself from school each Friday. Friday is the Moslem day of rest. The courts did not permit his objection to school attendance on Friday when based on the First Amendment's clauses. The court ordered he attend school on Fridays.[61] Other cases have been tried on similar grounds with the same conclusion, the First Amendment does not excuse one from school attendance.[62]

---

[58] *CIC.*, can. 1375.

[59] *CIC.*, can. 1322.

[60] *Watson v. Jones*, 80 U.S. 679, 20 L. Ed. 666; *United States v. Ballard*, 322 U.S. 78, 64 S. Ct. 882, 88 L. Ed. 1148 (1944); *West Virginia State Board of Education v. Barnett*, 319 U.S. 624, 68 S. Ct. 1178, 87 L. Ed. 1628.

[61] *Commonwealth v. Bey*, 116 Pa. Sup. 136, 70 Atl. 2d. 693 (1950).

[62] *Commonwealth v. Smoker*, 177 Pa. Sup. 435, 110 Atl. 2d. 740 (1955); *People ex. rel. Vollmar v. Stanley*, 81 Colo. 276, 255 P. 610 (1927).

The most frequent source of controversy in the educational field with respect to Constitutional provisions turns on the application of federal and state funds to private parochial schools. Some states have an express statute forbidding the application of public monies to private schools in any manner.[63] Other jurisdictions do not have such stringent regulations. Louisiana, for example, permits the distribution of textbooks to all students in the state, independently of the character of the institution they attend.[64] Mississippi concurs in the same practice.[65] The distribution of free textbooks is similar to the supplying of police and fire protection and bus transportation if designed to aid pupils as such. These practices all have a legitimate public purpose which does not violate the principles enunciated by the *Schempp* decision.[66] The Courts have maintained that the application of publicly raised tax funds in favor of a private parochial school does constitute a violation of the First Amendment.[67]

The Code of Canon Law does not demand financial support from the civil authorities for the support of ecclesiastical programs. The general law of the Church places the obligation of support upon the members of the Church. In demanding that the faithful support Church programs the universal law states that such a right is independent of the secular authority.[68]

While the weight of constitutional interpretation permits indirect aid to religious educational institutions,[69] the writer offers

---

[63] *Smith v. Donahue,* 202 N.Y. App. Div. 656, 195 N.Y. Supp. 715 (1922); *Donahoe v. Richards,* 38 Me. 376 (1854); *Dickman v. School District 62 c.,* 223 Ore. 347, 366 P. 2d. 533 (1961).

[64] *Cochrane v. Louisiana State Board of Education,* 281 U.S. 370, 50 S. Ct. 335, 74 L. Ed. 913 (1930).

[65] *Chance v. Mississippi State,* 190 Miss. 453, 200 S. 706 (1921).

[66] *School District of Abington Township v. Schempp,* 374 U.S. 203, 83 S. Ct. 1560, 10 L. Ed. 2d. 844.

[67] *Everson v. Board of Education,* 330 U.S. 1, 67 S. Ct. 504, 91 L. Ed. 711; *McCollum v. Board of Education,* 333 U.S. 203, 68 S. Ct. 461, 92 L. Ed. 649; *Swart v. South Burlington,* 122 Vt. 177, 167 Atl. 2d. 514 (1961); *Harfst v. Hoegen,* 349 Mo. 808, 163 S.W. 2d. 609 (1942).

[68] *CIC.,* can. 1496.

[69] *School District of Abington Township v. Schempp,* 374 U.S. 203, 83 S. Ct. 1560, 10 L. Ed. 2d. 844; *Zorach v. Clauson,* 343 U.S. 306, 72 S. Ct.

the following pattern as a possible means of securing direct aid to schools operated by religious associations, which pattern is within the boundaries of Constitutional limitations. At present many schools are directly owned by a parish, diocese, or religious society. If they are incorporated under the private eleemosynary statutes of the state and disassociated from the ownership of the parish, diocese or religious institute, the school could not be classified as a religious corporation. In its new corporate statutes the school would be merely a private corporation operating for an educational purpose, and aid to it as a secular institution would not as such be forbidden by the First Amendment. It could receive the support of taxes if there were no prohibition for the aid of a private school in the state's constitution.

The *Dartmouth*[70] case defined a corporation as a creature of the state.[71] Later in the *Bradfield v. Roberts* decision[72] the right of members of a particular religious group was vindicated to form a corporation. It was contended in the case under discussion that the incorporation of Providence Hospital of Washington, D. C., conducted by a religious community of women violated the establishment clause of the First Amendment. The hospital was so incorporated by an act of Congress in 1864. The United States Supreme Court stated

> Assuming that the hospital is a private eleemosynary corporation, the fact that its members . . . are members of a monastic order or sisterhood of the Roman Catholic Church, and the further fact that the hospital is conducted under the auspices of said church, are wholly immaterial.
>
> The facts above stated do not in the least change the legal character of the hospital, or make a religious corporation out of a purely secular one, as constituted by the law of its being. . . That the influence of any particular church may be powerful over the members of a nonsectarian and secular corporation, incorporated for a

679, 96 L. Ed. 954; *Everson v. Board of Education,* 330 U.S. 1, 67 S. Ct. 504, 91 L. Ed. 711; *Cochrane v. Louisiana State Board of Education,* 281 U.S. 370, 50 S. Ct. 335, 74 L. Ed. 913.

[70] *Dartmouth College v. Woodward,* N.H., 16 U.S. 518, 4 L. Ed. 629.

[71] *Supra,* pp. 88-89.

[72] *Bradfield v. Roberts,* 175 U.S. 291, 20 S. Ct. 121, 44 L. Ed. 168 (1899).

> definite purpose and with clearly stated powers, is surely not sufficient to convert such a corporation into a religious or sectarian body. . It is simply the case of a secular corporation being managed by people who hold to the doctrines of the Roman Catholic Church, but who nevertheless are managing the corporation according to the law under which it exists.[73]

The *Bradford* decision drew a distinction between the incorporators as citizens with civil rights and the same individuals as followers of a particular religious doctrine. The corporation is not made a religious corporation because of the belief of the members any more than any secular corporation does not become a religious corporation when the majority of the stockholders espouse one particular persuasion. The doctrine declared in the *Bradfield* decision has been followed in many subsequent decisions.[74]

The next case to be discussed in presenting a possible solution for securing tax aid flows from the decision of a Vermont court. In *Swart v. South Burlington*[75] a suit was instituted to enjoin a town from defraying the expenses of children when attending a parochial school. The Vermont court forbade the practice. The schools, so the record disclosed, were owned by the Roman Catholic Diocese of Burlington, Vermont. The courts recognized the importance of equity in the case, but nevertheless saw in the payment of tuition a violation of the First Amendment.

> The Church is the source of their control and the principal source of their support. This combination of factors renders the service of the Church and its ministry inseparable from its educational function. That this is a high and dedicated undertaking is not to be questioned,

---

[73] *Loc. cit.*

[74] *O'Leary v. Social Security Board,* 59 F. Supp. 997 (1945); *State v. Board of Trustees,* 175 Mo. 52, 74 S. W. 990 (1903); *Colbert v. Speer,* 24 App. D.C. 187 (1904) affirmed 200 U.S. 130, 25 S. Ct. 201, 50 L. Ed. 403 (1906); *Baltzell et al. v. Church Home and Infirmary of Baltimore City et al.,* 110 Md. 244, 73 Atl. 151 (1909); *Abernarthy v. City of Irbine, Ky.,* 355 S.W. 2d. 159 (1961).

[75] *Swart v. South Burlington,* 122 Vt. 177, 167 Atl. 2d. 514.

> and deserves the respect of all creeds. Yet, however worthy of the object, the First Amendment commands the State shall not participate.[76]

When the *Dartmouth* decision[77] is juxtaposed with the *Bradfield* decision[78] and the *Swart* case[79] it is evident that the belief of the corporation's members is not the determining factor regarding whether a corporation is a religious corporation. A religious corporation is defined in accordance with the articles of its incorporation. Now, should a school incorporate as a private eleemosynary corporation, admittedly with a preponderance of religious teachers but not owned by a religious corporation as such, then such an institution would not be a religious incorporation. The prescriptions of the definition of "establishment" given in the *Everson* decision[80] would not be applicable to the ensuing corporation. The school so incorporated could receive direct financial support if there be an enabling statute in the state constitution allowing for the expenditure of state money to a private educational institution.

SECTION 4. THE JUDICIAL DECISIONS OF ECCLESIASTICAL TRIBUNALS

Authority is clearly drawn in the visible society of the Catholic Church. The Pope as the successor of Saint Peter and Vicar of Christ on earth has supreme jurisdiction over the entire Church.[81] The bishops appointed by the Pontiff have the ordinary power over the churches entrusted to their care.[82] American civil law admits the position of these duly constituted sources of ecclesiastical authority. In the case of *Gonzalez v. the Archbishop of Manila*[83] the controversy turned around the proper authority

---

[76] *Loc. cit.*

[77] *Dartmouth College v. Woodward, N.H.*, 16 U.S. 518, 4 L. Ed. 629.

[78] *Bradfield v. Roberts,* 175 U.S. 291, 20 S. Ct. 121, 44 L. Ed. 168.

[79] *Swart v. South Burlington,* 122 Vt. 177, 167 Atl. 2d. 514.

[80] *Everson v. Board of Education,* 330 U.S. 1, 67 S. Ct. 504, 91 L. Ed. 711.

[81] *CIC.*, can. 218.

[82] *CIC.*, cans. 329, 335, § 1.

[83] *Gonzales v. Archbishop of Manila,* 280 U.S. 1, 50 S. Ct. 5, 74, L. Ed. 131 (1929).

of the Catholic Church to enact laws for its own concerns. The judiciary was asked to rule if Raul Rogerio Gonzalez was entitled to a chaplaincy. The appellant brought the action through his guardian to compel the Archbishop to confer upon him a chaplaincy as the legitimate heir to the office. The Supreme Court stated the Catholic Church had the native right to legislate concerning its own matters and to confer ecclesiastical offices only on those it recognizes as qualified in accordance with its own precepts. The Court stated in its opinion that the

> decision of the proper church tribunals on matters purely ecclesiastical, although affecting civil rights, are accepted in litigation before secular courts as conclusive.[84]

The Court decided the controversy in accordance with an earlier common law ruling of the same Supreme Court.

The *Watson v. Jones*[85] decision of the Supreme Court of the United States established the common law principle regarding the right of ecclesiastical judicial agencies to judge their own concerns. The Court was asked to settle the property interests of a Presbyterian church involved in an intra-church dispute. The General Assembly of the Presbyterian Church declared slavery sinful in 1861. The Presbytery of Louisville denounced the action as heretical. Many churches in fact did follow the Assembly's decree. The instant action was a result of the doctrinal controversy within one church, the Walnut Street Church. The Kentucky courts held that the pro-slavery members were the ones vested with the true property interests of the church. The Supreme Court overruled the Kentucky courts.

The Supreme Court classified churches with respect to their mode of internal government.

> [A] church of a strictly congregational or independent organization, is governed solely within itself, either by a majority of its members or by such other local organism as it may have substituted for the purposes of ecclesiastical

---

[84] *Loc. cit.*

[85] *Watson v. Jones*, 80 U.S. 679, 20 L. Ed. 666.

> government. [In such a church when there] . . is a schism . . the rights of such bodies to use the property must be determined by the ordinary principles which govern voluntary associations. . . . The minority, in choosing to separate themselves into a distinct body, can claim no rights in property from the fact that they had once been members of the church or congregation.[86]

The Court admitted there was another form of central authority in the ecclesiastical societies of the nation. The Supreme Court recognized the Presbyterian system of church government, i.e.

> one where there is . . . in regular succession the presbytery over the session or local church, the synod over the presbytery, and the General Assembly over all. . . .[87]

In the Presbyterian mode of organization the final arbiter of ecclesiastical issues is the highest ecclesiastical tribunal to which the controversy is brought. Since the church in question was one in the Presbyterian system, the civil courts were bound to recognize the decisions of that church's judiciary agencies.

The *Watson* decision was the foundation of the federal common law.[88] It must be noted that the Court in handing down its ruling based the decision on common law, not on the application of the First and Fourteenth Amendments.[89] The decision, it is true, was binding on all federal courts, but in itself the decision did not necessarily bind state courts.[90] Many states did follow the *Watson* ruling,[91] but many did not accept the binding force of ecclesiastical tribunals regarding cases dealing with property interests.[92]

---

[86] *Loc. cit.*

[87] *Loc. cit.*

[88] "Comments," *New York Law Review,* XXXV (1960), 1371-1372.

[89] "Comments," *Columbia Law Review,* LIV (1956), 436.

[90] Bergman, "Recent Cases," *University of Cincinnati Law Review,* XXII (1953), 247.

[91] *Krecker v. Shirley,* 163 Pa. 534, 30 Atl. 440 (1894); *Baxter v. McDonnell,* 155 N.Y. 83, 49 N.E. 667 (1898); *Carter v. Papineau, 222* Mass. 464, 111 N.E. 358.

[92] *State ex. re. Soares v. Hebrew Congregation,* 31 La. App. 205, 33 Am. Rep. 217 (1879); *Schlichter v. Keitter,* 156 Pa. 119, 27 Atl. 45 (1893); *Olear v. Haniak,* 235 Mo. App. 249, 131 S.W. 2d. 375 (1939).

The dilemma regarding the binding force of church courts was finally settled in *Kedroff v. St. Nicholas Cathedral.*[93] The case arose from a schism within the Russian Orthodox Church. There was an ecclesiastical reaction to the Communist party's alleged domination of the Russian Orthodox Church, whose principal governing body is located in Moscow. Some churchmen in the United States believed that the Moscow Patriarchate was completely dominated by the Soviet government. To combat the political and atheistic intrusions the American churchmen established the Metropolitan of All America and Canada. The new body was to care for all the Russian Orthodox faithful until such time that the Patriarch should be able to exercise independent control and action as the supreme authority of Russian Orthodoxy. New York State added an amendment to its religious corporation laws stabilizing the new ecclesiastical body within its jurisdiction.

A minority of Russian Orthodox churchmen in the United States retained their allegiance to the Patriarch. They challenged the New York statute as an unwarranted invasion of their free exercise of religion under the First Amendment of the Federal Constitution. The Russian Orthodox authorities in Moscow ordered a new sober or council to be held in the United States to formally reunite the diocese in the United States with the Russian Mother Church. The majority of the congregations in America, speaking through their Sober held in Cleveland in 1946, refused to comply with the Moscow order. They further declared

> . . that any administrative recognition of the Synod of the Russian Orthodox Church abroad is terminated, retaining however, our spiritual and brotherly relations with all parts of the Russian Orthodox Church abroad.[94]

The minority group sought civilly to vindicate their proper possession of the Cathedral situated in New York City. They

---

[93] *Kedroff v. St. Nicholas Cathedral,* 344 U.S. 94, 73 S. Ct. 143, 97 L. Ed. 120 (1952).

[94] *Loc. cit.*

brought their case on appeal to the Supreme Court which ruled as follows:

> This controversy concerning the right to use Saint Nicholas Cathedral is strictly a matter of ecclesiastical government, the power of the Supreme Court Authority of the Russian Orthodox Church to appoint the ruling hierarch of the archdiocese of North America. . . . Ours is a government which by the "law of its being" allows no statute, state or national, that prohibits the free exercise of religion. There are occasions when civil courts must draw lines between the responsibilities of church and state for the disposition or use of property. Even in those cases when the property right follows as an incident from the decisions of the church custom or law on ecclesiastical issues, the church rule controls. This under our Constitution necessarily follows in order that there may be free exercise of religion.[95]

The *Kedroff* decision settled the ambiguities of the *Watson* case.[96] The Kedroff decision was binding on all courts, federal and civil. Through the application of the Fourteenth Amendment the state courts were no longer free to accept or reject the common law doctrine. *Kedroff* raised the common law opinion to a constitutional doctrine.[97] Henceforth the settlement of religious controversies, whether of doctrine, of office holders, or of property interests, must be adjudicated in accordance with the principles of the denomination. Should the particular church be structured hierarchically as is the Roman Catholic Church, the decision given by the ecclesiastical tribunal will bind the civil courts. What the courts have done is to treat religious questions as they would treat the internal disputes of any private association. The association's by-laws would be the controlling principles upon the courts; the religious society's principles in like fashion are the court's controlling principles.[98]

---

[95] *Loc. cit.*

[96] *Watson v. Jones,* 80 U.S. 679, 20 L. Ed. 666.

[97] "Comments," *Columbia Law Review,* LIV (1956), 436.

[98] *Harvard Law Review,* LXVII (1935), 1110: "In giving this principle constitutional significance, while extending it to include executive appointments by a hierarchy and in holding that it bars even legislatively approved

In spite of the explicit statements of the Supreme Court together with the legal opinions, another attempt was made to circumvent the *Kedroff* ruling. The courts of New York ruled that they were not bound by the *Kedroff* decision. New York's courts held that the right conferred under the canon law of the Orthodox Church to use the St. Nicholas Cathedral was not binding on that state's judicial system. The Court of Appeals, the highest judicial agency in New York, ruled that by virtue of the domination of the Soviet government over the Russian Orthodox Patriarch, the appointments of that ecclesiastical dignitary were not binding in the common law of New York. The United States Supreme Court answered this challenge to its authority in *Kreshik v. St. Nicholas Cathedral of the Russian Orthodox Church of North America.*[99] The Supreme Court reversed the Court of Appeals decision. The opinion of the Supreme Court read in part:

> It is not of moment that the state has here acted solely through its judicial branch, for whether legislative or judicial, it is still the application of state power which we are asked to scrutinize. . . . Accordingly, our ruling in Kedroff is controlling here and requires dismissal of the complaint.[100]

The *Kedroff* and *Kreshik* decisions are of great practical importance for the Roman Catholic Church. The civil rulings reaffirm the constitutional rights of the Church to enact its proper regulations for the membership of the Church. The Church is civilly recognized as the proper regulatory agency in matters of Catholic doctrine and discipline. The supernatural right of the

---

schisms the present Court has taken a major step to insure the maximum autonomy of church governments within the civil framework. If the principle also freezes control of church property in favor of dominant hierarchy, this preservation of the *status quo* seems to be in accord with the original donors of the property. . . . Thus the present decision merely commands that once the nature of the church structure and legitimacy of those holding office in it are established, the state should not substitute its own laws for the church in disposing of church property.

[99] *Kreshik v. St. Nicholas Cathedral of the Russian Orthodox Church of North America,* 363 U.S. 190, 83 S. Ct. 1583, 10 L. Ed. 2d. 871 (1960).

[100] *Loc. cit.*

Church to be the teacher and ruler of the faithful is guaranteed in accordance with principles of natural justice.

Without realizing it New York State's actions in the *Kedroff* and *Kreshik* cases was an attempt to set back the course of religious liberty in the United States to the days prior to the Federal Constitution. The judicial decisions of that State in effect relegated the Church to the position of an arm of the secular authority. Should New York's ruling have been left standing, it would have meant that secular authorities would have the right to determine what would be the proper structures and authorities within any religious group. The State of New York had moved into that area of religious liberty which Thomas Jefferson declared to be the sole right of the citizen.[101] The Supreme Court in overturning New York's decisions reinforced the proper and exclusive right of the Roman Catholic Church and every religious society to proclaim its own policy and its own form of government. The rights of the Church, although not recognized constitutionally as divine prerogatives, are nevertheless secured through the natural law application of the Constitution of the United States against all intrusions by any secular power or authority.

---

[101] *Supra*, p. 44, footnote n. 7.

CONCLUSIONS

1. The Constitution of the United States of America is an instrument whereby the people of the United States confer powers on the federal institutions and government. The people did not give the federal government any power to legislate concerning matters of religion as such. In this the democratic institutions and practices of the United States differ from the "liberal" democracies of nineteenth century Europe.

2. The Federal Constitution applies the same limitations to the states as is applied to federal branches of government concerning religious matters.

3. The Roman Catholic Church, established by the will of Jesus Christ, is a true, juridic, perfect society and as such may confer corporate or moral personality on the associations of its faithful.

4. The Establishment clause of the First Amendment to the Constitution of the United States requires that the agencies of federal and state governments must hold themselves neutral with reference to religious institutions. The governments of the United States and the respective states may pass any legislation that indirectly aids religious institutions, provided the direct and immediate purpose of the said legislation is publicly orientated.

5. The form of democracy reviewed by early papal pronouncements did not reflect the democratic institutions of the United States. The papal demand that the state specifically recognize the existence of the Roman Catholic Church referred to a form of democracy known as paternalism. Since the United States is not a paternalistic democracy, it was not bound to specifically recognize the Roman Catholic Church.

6. Papal teachings and the decrees of Vatican II proclaim the right of each individual to worship God in accordance with the dictates of each one's conscience. This right is the right of each

human being. The constitutional guarantees of freedom of religion in the United States conforms to this natural right.

7. The Roman Catholic Church may not be recognized in the United States for the reason that the First Amendment places a restriction on the federal government, and because the theory of corporations as espoused by the common law of the United States holds that all natural moral unions, if they are to have a formal corporate existence, must be so created by the states.

8. No form of incorporation practiced in the United States is in perfect conformity with the dictates of Canon Law; but, the Sacred Congregation of the Council has directed that, wherever possible, the goods of ecclesiastical moral personalities should be held in the form of the corporation aggregate.

9. The United States of America has had diplomatic relations with the Papal States, and later recognized the corporate character of the Holy See in those territories which were ceded to the United States by the Treaty of Paris which concluded the Spanish American War. The Holy See is an accredited observer to the United Nations and serves on various committees thereon with the United States of America.

10. The Constitution of the United States insures to the Church its right to preach and to conduct schools. This right is based, not on the supernatural character of the Church, but on the natural right of all religions to exist and disseminate their doctrines.

11. The judicial decisions of the Roman Catholic Church tribunals are accepted by the civil courts in the United States as binding even when such decisions affect property interests. At first this binding status of ecclesiastical judgments was part of the federal common law, but since 1952 the binding force of the Church's tribunals is part of the rights secured by the Constitution of the United States.

BIBLIOGRAPHY

Sources

Acta Apostolicae Sedis, Commentarium Officiale, Romae: 1909-1929; Civitate Vaticana, 1929-

Acta et Decreta Concilii Plenarii Baltimorensis III (1884), Baltimorae, Typis Ioannis Murphy et Sociorum, 1886.

Annals of Congress, The Debates and Proceeding in Congress of the United States, First to the Eighteenth Congress, Washington, D. C.: Gales and Seaton, 1834.

Acta Sanctae Sedis, 41 vols., Romae, 1865-1908.

Bouscaren, T. Lincoln, O'Connor, James I., *The Canon Law Digest,* 5 vols., Milwaukee: Bruce Publishing Co., Vol. I, 1934; Vol. II, 1943; Vol. III, 1954; edited by Bouscaren and O'Connor: Vol. IV, 1958; Vol. V, 1963.

Bruns, H., *Canones Apostolorum et Conciliorum Saeculorum IV-VII,* 2 vols., Berolini, 1839.

Codex, Iuris Canonici Pii X Pontificis Maximi iussi digestus, Benedicti Papae XV auctoritate promulgatus, Romae: Typis Polyglottis Vaticanis, 1917.

Codex Iuris Canonici Orientalis, Pro Ecclesia Orientalibus adnotationibus fontium actus cura Pontificii Consilii Codici Iuris Canonici Orientalis redigendo: *Litterae Apostolicae Crebrae Allatae,* motu proprio datae, 22 febr. 1949; *Litterae Apostolicae Sollicitudinem Nostram,* motu proprio datae, 6 ian. 1950; *Litterae Apostolicae Postquam Apostolicis,* motu proprio datae, 9 febr. 1952; *Litterae Apostolicae Cleri Sanctitate,* motu proprio datae, 11 iun. 1957.

Congressional Globe, The Proceedings and Debates of the Twenty-Third to the Forty-Second Congress, Washington, D. C.: Globe Office, 1834-1873.

Congressional Record, Proceedings and Debates of the Forty-Third Congress to the Present, Washington, D. C.: United States Printing Office, 1874-

Corpus Iuris Civilis, 3 vols., Vol. I, *Institutiones,* ed. stereotypa quintadecima, quas recognovit P. Kraeger; Vol. II, *Codex Iustinianus,* ed. stereotypa decima, recognovit, et retractavit, P. Krueger; Vol. III, *Novellae,* ed. stereotypa quinta, quas recognovit R. Schoell et absolvit G. Kroll, Berolini: Apud Weidmannos, 1928-1929.

Corwin, Edward S., *The Constitution of the United States of America, Analysis and Interpretation,* Washington, D. C.: United States Printing Office, 1952.

Labbeus, P. Cossartius, G., *Sacrosancta Concilia ad Regiam Editionem Exacta,* 17 vols. in 18, Parisiis, 1671-1674.

Mansi, J., *Sacrorum Conciliorum Nova et Amplissima Collectio,* 53 vols. in 60, Parisiis, 1901-1927.

Reference Works

Abbo, John-Hannan, Jerome D., *The Sacred Canons,* 2 vols., revised edition, St. Louis, Mo.: B. Herder Book Co., 1957.

Antieau, Chester James-Downey, Arthur T.-Roberts, Edward, *Freedom from Federal Establishment,* Milwaukee: Bruce Publishing Company, 1964.

Augustine, Charles A., *A Commentary on the New Code of Canon Law,* 8 vols., Vol. VI, 2. ed., St. Louis: B. Herder Book Co., 1923.

Baart, Peter A., *The Tenure of Catholic Church Property in the United States of America,* Marshall, Michigan: The Author, 1900.

Bartlett, Chester J., *The Tenure of Parochial Property in the United States of America,* The Catholic University of America Canon Law Studies, n. 31, Washington, D. C.: The Catholic University of America, 1926.

Beard, Charles A., *The Supreme Court and the Constitution,* New York: The Paisley Press, Inc., 1938.

Bertrams, Wilhelm, *The Papacy, the Episcopacy, and Collegiality,* Westminster, Maryland: The Newman Press, 1964.

Beste, Udalricus, *Introductio in Codicem,* 5. ed., Neapoli: M d'Auria, 1961.

Black, Henry Campbell, *Law Dictionary,* 3. ed., St. Paul: West Publishing Co., 1933.

Blackstone, Sir William, *Commentaries on the Laws of England,* 4 vols., New York, 1852.

Blat, Albertus, *Commentarium Textus Codicis Iuris Canonici,* 5 vols. in 7, Vol. II, 2. ed., 1921, Romae: Ex Typographia Pontificia in Institutio Pii IX, 1921.

Boffa, Conrad, *Canonical Provisions for Catholic Schools,* The Catholic University of America Canon Law Studies, n. 117, Washington, D. C.: The Catholic University of America Press, 1939.

Bouscaren, T. Lincoln, Ellis, Adam C., *Canon Law, A Text and Commentary,* 2. ed., Milwaukee: The Bruce Publishing Company, 1951.

Bouvier, John, *Law Dictionary,* 2 vols., Boston, 1897.

Brown, Brendan, *The Canonical Juristic Personality with Special Reference to Its Status in the United States of America,* The Catholic University of America Studies in Canon and Civil Law, n. 39, Washington, D. C.: The Catholic University of America, 1927.

Cappello, Felix, *Summa Iuris Publici Ecclesiastici,* 6. ed., Romae: Ades Universitatis Gregorianae, 1954.

Cleary, Joseph F., *Canonical Limitations on the Alienation of Church Property,* The Catholic University of America Canon Law Studies, n. 100, Washington, D. C.: The Catholic University of America, 1936.

Colomer, Luis, Rockey, Palmer L., *The Catholic Church: The Mystical Body of Christ,* Paterson, N. J.: St. Anthony Guild Press, 1952.

Comyns, Joseph L., *Papal and Episcopal Administration of Church Property,* The Catholic University of America Canon Law Studies, n. 147, Washington, D. C.: The Catholic University of America Press, 1942.

Conte a Coronata, Matthaeus, *Institutiones Iuris Canonici,* 4 vols., Vols. I-III, 4. ed., Vol. IV, 3 ed., Taurini, Marietti, 1950-1956.

Costanzo, Joseph, *This Nation Under God,* New York: Herder & Herder, 1964.

De Pauw, Gommar Albert, *The Legal Status of Catholic Elementary Schools in Belgium, 1830-1950,* The Catholic University of America Canon Law Studies, n. 336, Washington, D. C.: The Catholic University of America Press, 1953.

Dignan, Patrick J., *A History of the Legal Incorporation of Catholic Church Property in the United States,* New York: Kennedy and Sons, 1935.

Dninan, Robert, *Religion, the Courts and Public Policy,* New York: McGraw-Hill Book Company, Inc., 1963.

Doheny, William J., *Church Property: Modes of Acquisition,* The Catholic University of America Canon Law Studies, n. 41, Washington, D. C.: The Catholic University of America, 1927.

Fagannus, Prosper, *Commentaria in Libros Decretalium,* 8 vols. in 5, Venetiis: apud Paulum Balleonium, 1697.

Fleming, Peter, *The Laws of the State of Minnesota Affecting Church Property,* The Catholic University of America Canon Law Studies, n. 438, Washington, D. C., microfilm, 1964.

Feiertag, Sister Loretta Clare, *American Public Opinion on the Diplomatic Relations between the United States and the Papal States (1847-1867),* Graduate School of Arts and Science of the Catholic University of America, Washington, D. C.: The Catholic University of America, 1933.

Fournier, Paul Eugene Louis, *Les Officialités au Moyen Age,* Paris: E. Plon et Cie, 1880.

Gargan, Edward T., *Leo XIII and the Modern World,* New York: Sheed and Ward, 1961.

Gierke, Otto Frederick, Maitland, Frederic William, *Political Theories of the Middle Ages,* Cambridge University Press, 1900.

Gilligan, Withbread, *The Development of the Idea of Judicial Review,* New York: Columbia University, Master Thesis, 1954.

Gilson, Etieene, *The Church Speaks to the Modern World,* Garden City, N. Y.: Image Books, 1954.

Goodwine, John A., *The Right of the Church to Acquire Temporal Goods,* The Catholic University of America Canon Law Studies, n. 131, Washington, D. C.: The Catholic University of America Press, 1941.

Graham, Robert A., *Vatican Diplomacy, A Study of Church and State on the International Plane,* Princeton, N. J.: Princeton University Press, 1959.

Guthrie, William D., *Lectures on the Fourteenth Article of the Amendment to the Constitution of the United States,* Boston: Little, Brown and Company, 1898.

Hamilton, Alexander-Madison, James-Jay, John, *The Federalist,* Earle, ed., New York: Random House, 1937.

Heston, Edward L., *The Alienation of Church Property in the United States,* The Catholic University of America Canon Law Studies, n. 132, Washington, D. C.: The Catholic University of America Press, 1941.

Hinschius, Paul, *System des katholischen Kirchenrechts,* 6 vols., Berlin: 1869-1897.

Hirschfeld, Robert S., *The Constitution of the Court, The Development of the Basic Law Through Judicial Interpretation,* New York: Random House, 1962.

Jackson, Robert Houghwont, *The Struggle for Judicial Supremacy—A Study of a Crisis in American Power Politics,* New York: Alfred A. Knopf, 1941.

Jansen, Raymond, *Canonical Provision for Catechetical Instruction,* The Catholic University of America Canon Law Studies, n. 107, Washington, D. C.: The Catholic University of America, 1937.

Kauper, Paul G., *Religion and the Constitution,* Kingsport, Tenn.: Louisiana State University Press, 1964.

Kent, James, *Commentaries on American Law,* 4 vols., ed. by O. W. Holmes, 13 ed., Charles M. Barnes, Boston: Little, Brown and Company, 1884.

Kerwin, Jerome G., *Catholic Viewpoint on Church and State,* Garden City, N. J.: Hanover House, 1960.

Kilcullen, Thomas J., *The Collegiate Moral Person as Party Litigant,* The Catholic University of America Canon Law Studies, n. 251, Washington, D. C.: The Catholic University of America Press, 1947.

Kremer, Michael N., *Church Support in the United States,* The Catholic University of America Canon Law Studies, n. 61, Washington, D. C.. The Catholic University of America, 1930.

Kurland, Philip B., *Religion and the Law,* Chicago. Aldine Publishing Company, 1961.

Kurtscheid, Bertrandus, *Historia Iuris Canonici, Historia Institutorum,* 2. ed., Romae: Officum Libri Catholici, 1951.

Lamott, John Henry, *History of the Archdiocese of Cincinnati,* New York: Frederick Pustet Co., 1921.

Marnell, William H., *First Amendment,* Garden City, N. Y.: Doubleday & Company, Inc., 1964.

Mason, Alpheus T., Beany, William M., *American Constitutional Law,* Englewood Cliffs, N. J.: Prentice Hall, Inc., 1954.

McGough, James Patrick, *The Laws of the State of Mississippi Affecting Church Property,* The Catholic University of America Canon Law Studies, n. 417, Washington, D. C.: The Catholic University of America Press, 1962.

McLeaish, Donald, *The Laws of the State of Texas Affecting Church Property,* The Catholic University of America Canon Law Studies, n. 405, Washington, D. C.: The Catholic University of America Press, 1960.

McLoughlin, Peter, *The Constitution of the United States,* Doctoral Presentation to the Faculty of Law, Catholic University of America, Washington, D. C., no date given.

Michiels, Gommarus, *Principia Generalia de Personis in Ecclesia, 2.* ed., Parisiis-Tornaci-Romae: Desclée, 1955.

Murphy, Joseph, *The Laws of the State of New York Affecting Church Property,* The Catholic University of America Canon Law Studies, n. 388, Washington, D. C.: The Catholic University of America Press, 1957.

Murray, John Courtney, *We Hold These Truths,* New York: Sheed and Ward, 1960.

Navarrus, *Opera Omnia,* 6 vols., Venetiis, 1618.

Nessel, William, *First Amendment Freedoms, Papal Pronouncements and Concordat Practice,* The Catholic University of America Canon Law Studies, n. 142, The Catholic University of America Press, 1961.

O'Brien, F. William, *Mr. Justice Reed and the First Amendment,* Washington, D. C.: Georgetown University Press, 1958.

Olalia, Alexander, *A Comparative Study of the Christian Constitution of States and the Constitution of the Philippine Commonwealth,* The Catholic University of America Canon Law Studies, n. 206, Washington, D. C.: The Catholic University of America Press, 1944.

Oppenheimer, L., *International Law,* 2 vols., 8. ed., Vol. I, 1954, Vol. II, 1955, London: Longmans.

O'Toole, Thomas J., *Institute of Church and State Proceedings,* Villanova School of Law, Villanova, Pa., 1958.

Pfeffer, Leo, *The Liberties of an American,* Boston: Beacon Press, 1956.

Pollock, F.-Maitland, F., *History of English Law,* 2 vols., 2. ed., Cambridge: University Press, 1909.

Pritchett, C. Herman, *The American Constitutional System,* New York: McGraw-Hill Book Company, Inc., 1963.

Rahner, Carl-Ratzinger, Joseph, *The Episcopate and the Primacy,* New York: Herder & Herder, 1962.

Regan, Richard J., *American Pluralism and the Catholic Conscience,* New York: Macmillan Company, 1963.

Regatillo, Eduardo, *Institutiones Iuris Canonici,* 2 vols., 6. ed., Santander: Sal Terra, 1961.

Rice, Charles E., *The Supreme Court and Public Prayer,* New York: Fordham University Press, 1964.

Rodriques, Manuel, *The Laws of the State of New Mexico Affecting Church Property,* The Catholic University of America Canon Law Studies, n. 406, Washington, D. C.: The Catholic University of America Press, 1959.

St. Thomas Aquinas, *Summa Theologicae,* 5 vols., Taurini: Marietti, 1932.

Schierse, Paul, *Laws of the State of Delaware Affecting Church Property,* The Catholic University of America Canon Law Studies, n. 428, Washington, D. C.: The Catholic University of America Press, 1963.

Shoup, Earl L., *The National Government of the American People,* Boston: Ginn and Company, 1948.

Schroeder, Henry J., *Canons and Decrees of the Council of Trent,* St. Louis, Mo.: B. Herder Book Co., 1941.

Stokes, Anson Phelps, *Church and State in the United States,* 3 vols., New York: Harper & Brothers, 1950.

Suarez, Franciscus, *Opera Omnia,* 28 vols. in 30, Parisiis, 1856-1878.

Torpey, William George, *Judicial Doctrines of Religious Rights in America,* Chapel Hill: The University of North Carolina Press, 1948.

Tussman, Joseph, *The Supreme Court on Church and State,* New York: Oxford University Press, 1962.

Tyler, R. H., *American Ecclesiastical Law,* Albany, N. Y., 1886.

Van Epsen, Zeger, *Ius Ecclesiasticum Universum,* 5 vols., Louvanii, 1753.

Vromant, G., *De Bonis Temporalibus,* 3. ed., Bruges-Paris: Desclée de Brouwer, 1953.

Welsh, Maurice, *The Laws of the State of Nevada Affecting Church Property,* The Catholic University of America Canon Law Studies, n. 409, Washington, D. C.: The Catholic University of America Press, 1962.

Wernz, F., Vidal, P., *Ius Canonicum ad Normam Codicis Exactam,* 7 vols., in 8, Vol. II, 3. ed., Romae: Apud Ades Universitatis Gregorianae, 1943.

Wiggins, Urban C., *Property Laws of the State of Ohio Affecting Church Property,* The Catholic University of America Canon Law Studies, n. 367, Washington, D. C.: The Catholic University of America Press, 1956.

Woywod, Stanislaus, Smith, Callistus, *A Practical Commentary on the Code of Canon Law,* 2 vols. in 1, revised ed., New York: Joseph F. Wagner, Inc., 1957.

Zollmann, Carl, *American Church Law,* St. Paul: West Publishing Co., 1933.

Articles Used

Bergman, Milton, "Recent Cases," *University of Cincinnati Law Review,* XXII (1953), 246-250.

Clark, Tom C., "Religion and the Law," *South Carolina Law Review,* XV (1963), 855-866.

"Comments," *Columbia Law Review,* LIV (1956), 435-438.

———, *Harvard Law Review,* LXVII (1953), 1109-1112.

———, *New York University Law Review,* XXXV (1960), 1370-1375.

Connell, Francis J., "The Relationship between Church and State," *Jurist,* XIII (1953), 398-414.

"Constitutional Law, Freedom of Religion," *Harvard Law Review,* LXVII (1957), 109-112.

Dunsforth, John E., "The Establishment Syndrome and Religious Liberty," *Duquesne Law Review,* II (1964), 139-212.

Eberger, Carl F., "Recent Decision," *Notre Dame Lawyer,* XXXVIII (1953), 338-405.

Fellman, D., "Religion in American Public Law," *Boston University Law Review,* XLIV (1964), 287-399.

"The Free Exercise and Establishment Clause, Note," *Minnesota Law Review,* XLVIII (1964), 929-946.

Kauper, Paul G., "Separation of Church and State—A Constitutional View," *Catholic Lawyer,* IX (1963), 32-42.

———, "The Supreme Court and the Rule of Law," *Michigan Law Review,* LIX (1960), 531-552.

Kurland, Philip B., "Of Church and State and the Supreme Court," *The University of Chicago Law Review,* XXIX (1961), 1-96.

Klinkhamer, Sister Mary Carolyn, "Blaine Amendment of 1875: Private Motives for Political Action," *Catholic Historical Review,* XLII (1956), 15-49.

McGrath, John J., "Canon Law and American Church Law: A Comparative Study," *Jurist,* XVIII (1958), 260-278.

Meyer, Alfred W., "The Blaine Amendment and the Bill of Rights," *Harvard Law Review,* LXIV (1951), 939-945.

Moore, John Norton, "Supreme Court and the Relationship between 'Establishment' and 'Free Exercise' Clauses," *Texas Law Review,* XLII (1963), 142-198.

Murray, John Courtney, "The Problem of Pluralism in America," *Thought,* XXIX (1954), 165-208.

———, "Leo XIII: Separation of Church and State," *Theological Studies,* XIV (1953), 145-214.

———, "Leo XIII: Two Concepts of Government," *Theological Studies,* XIV (1953), 551-567.

Slough, M. C., McAnany, T. C., "Governmental Aid to Church Related Schools: An Analysis," *Kansas Law Review,* XI (1962), 35-75.

Sutherland, Arthur E., "Establishment according to Engel," *Harvard Law Review,* LXXVI (1962), 25-52.

Weclew, Robert C., "The Establishment Clause and Coercion," *Marquette Law Review,* XLVII (1963), 359-367.

PERIODICALS USED

Boston University Law Review, Worcester, Mass., 1921-

Catholic Historical Review, Washington, D. C., 1918-

Catholic Lawyer, Brooklyn, N. Y., 1955-

Clergy Review, London, 1931-
Columbia Law Review, New York, 1900-
Duquesne Law Review, Pittsburgh, Pa., 1963-
Harvard Law Review, Cambridge, Mass., 1887-
Jurist, Washington, D. C., 1941-
Marquette Law Review, Milwaukee, Wis., 1916-
Michigan Law Review, Ann Arbor, Mich., 1892-
Minnesota Law Review, St. Paul, Minn., 1893-1916.
———, Minneapolis, Minn., 1917-
New York University Law Review, New York, 1928-
Notre Dame Law Review, South Bend, Ind., 1925-
The Pope Speaks, Chevy Chase, Md., 1954-
South Carolina Law Review, Columbia, South Carolina, 1948-
Texas Law Review, Austin, Texas, 1922-
Theological Studies, New York, 1940-
Thought, New York, 1926-
University of Cincinnati Law Review, Cincinnati, Ohio, 1927-
University of Kansas Law Review, Lawrence, Kansas, 1952-

Table of Cases

Abernathy v. City of Irbine, 355 S.W. 2d. 159 (1961).

Anderson-Tully Co. v. Gillett Lumber Company, 155 Ark. 224, 244 S.W. 26 (1922).

Baltzell et al. v. Church Home and Infirmary of Baltimore City et al., 110 Md. 244, 73 Atl. 151 (1909).

Baptist Church v. Witherell, 11 N.Y. 296 (1832).

Barron v. Baltimore, 32 U.S. 245, 8 L. Ed. 672 (1833).

Baxter v. McDonnell, 155 N.Y. 83, 49 N.E. 667 (1898).

Bloom v. Richards, 2 Ohio 387 (1853).

Bradfield v. Roberts, 175 U.S. 291, 20 S. Ct. 121, 44 L. Ed. 168 (1899)

Bridges v. Wilson, 58 Tenn. 458 (1872).

Cantwell v. Connecticut, 310 U.S. 296, 60 S. Ct. 980, 84 L. Ed. 1213 (1940).

Carter v. Papineau, 222 Mass. 464, 111 N.E. 358 (1916).

Chance v. Mississippi State, 190 Miss. 453, 200 So. 706 (1921).

Chaplinsky v. New Hampshire, 315 U.S. 568, 62 S. Ct. 766, 86 L. Ed. 1031 (1942).

Cleveland v. United States, 329 U.S. 14, 67 S. Ct. 13, 91 L. Ed. 12 (1946).

Cochrane v. Louisiana State Board of Education, 281 U.S. 370, 50 S. Ct. 335, 74 L. Ed. 913 (1930).

Colbert v. Speer, 24 App. D.C. 187 (1904) ; affirmed 200 U.S. 130, 26 S. Ct. 201, 50 L. Ed. 403 (1906).

Commonwealth v. Bey, 116 Pa. Sup. 136, 70 Atl. 2d. 693 (1950).

Commonwealth v. Smoker, 177 Pa. Sup. 435, 110 Atl. 2d. 740 (1955).

Cox v. New Hampshire, 312 U.S. 569, 61 S. Ct. 762, 85 L. Ed. 1049 (1941).

Dartmouth College v. Woodward, N.H., 16 U. S. 518, 4 L. Ed. 629 (1819).

Davis v. Beason, 133 U.S. 333, 10 S. Ct. 299, 33 L. Ed. 637 (1890).

Dickman v. School District 62 c, 223 Ore. 347, 366 P. 2d. 533 (1961).

Donahoe v. Richards, 38 Me. 376 (1854).

Douglas v. City of Jeanette, 319 U.S. 157, 63 S. Ct. 877, 87 L. Ed. 1324 (1943).

Earle v. Wood, 62 Mass. 430 (1851).

Ellis v. State, 10 Ala. App. 252, 65 So. 412 (1914).

Engel v. Vitale, 370 U.S. 421, 82 S. Ct. 1261, 8 L. Ed. 2d. 601 (1962).

Everson v. Board of Education, 330 U.S. 1, 67 S. Ct. 504, 91 L. Ed. 711 (1947).

Feiner v. New York, 340 U.S. 315, 71 S. Ct. 303, 95 L. Ed. 295 (1951).

Fitzgerald v. Robinson, 112 Mass. 371 (1873).

Gitlow v. New York, 268 U.S. 652, 45 S. Ct. 625, 69 L. Ed. 1138 (1925).

Gonzalez v. Archbishop of Manila, 280 U.S. 1, 50 S. Ct. 5, 74 L. Ed. 131 (1929).

Hague v. C.I.O., 307 U.S. 469, 59 S. Ct. 954, 83 L. Ed. 1423 (1939).

Hale v. Everett, 53 N.H. 9, 16 Am. Rep. 82 (1902).

Harfst v. Hoegen, 349 Mo. 808, 163 S.W. 2d. 609 (1942).

Hundley v. Collins, 131 Ala. 234, 32 S. 575 (1902).

In Re Jenison, 375 U.S. 14, 84 S. Ct. 136, 11 L. Ed. 2d. 45 (1963).

In the matter of Mt. Sinai Hospital, 250 N.Y. 103, 164 N.E. 871 (1928).

Jamison v. State of Texas, 318 U.S. 415, 63 S. Ct. 669, 87 L. Ed. 869 (1943).

Jones v. State, 28 Neb. 495, 44 N.W. 658 (1890).

Kedroff v. St. Nicholas Cathedral, 344 U.S. 94, 73 S. Ct. 143, 97 L. Ed. 120 (1952).

Kinney v. State, 38 Ala. 224 (1862).

Klix v. Polish Roman Catholic Church St. Stanislaus Parish, 137 Mo. App. 347, 118 S.W. 1171 (1901).

Kovacs v. Cooper, 336 U.S. 77, 69 S. Ct. 448, 93 L. Ed. 513 (1949).

Krecker v. Shirley, 163 Pa. 534, 30 Atl. 440 (1894).

Kreshik v. St. Nicholas Cathedral of the Russian Orthodox Church of North America, 363 U.S. 190, 83 S. Ct. 1583, 10 L. Ed. 2d. 871 (1960).

Kunz v. New York, 340 U.S. 290, 71 S. Ct. 312, 95 L. Ed. 280 (1951).

Love v. State, 35 Tex. Crim. 27, 29 S.W. 790 (1895).

Mannix v. Purcell, 46 Ohio 102 (1888).

Marbury v. Madison, 5 U.S. 368, 2 L. Ed. 60 (1803).

Marchman v. McCoy Hospital Operating Co., 21 S.W. 2d. 552 (1929).

Marsh v. Alabama, 326 U.S. 501, 66 S. Ct. 276, 90 L. Ed. 265 (1946).

Martin v. City of Struthers, 319 U.S. 141, 63 S. Ct. 862, 87 L. Ed. 1313 (1943).

McCollum v. Board of Education, 333 U.S. 203, 68 S. Ct. 461, 92 L. Ed. 649 (1948).

McCullough v. Maryland, 16 U.S. 316, 4 L. Ed. 579 (1819).

McGinnis v. Watson, 41 Pa. 9 (1861).

McGowan v. State of Maryland, 366 U.S. 420, 81 S. Ct. 1101, 6 L. Ed. 2d. 393 (1961).

McNeilly v. First Baptist Church of Brookline, 243 Mass. 331, 137 N.E. 691 (1923).

Miller v. Baptist Church, 16 N.J.L. 251 (1837).

Morgan v. Rose, 22 N.J.Eq. 583 (1871).

Municipality of Ponce v. Roman Catholic Apostolic Church in Puerto Rico, 210 U.S. 296, 28 S. Ct. 737, 52 L. Ed. 1068 (1908).

Murdock v. Pennsylvania, 319 U.S. 105, 63 S. Ct. 891, 87 L. Ed. 1292 (1943).

New Colonial Ice Co. v. Helvering, 294 U.S. 435, 55 S. Ct. 440, 79 L. Ed. 977 (1934).

New Hampshire v. Hoyt, 84 N.H. 38, 146 Atl. 170 (1929).

Olear v. Haniak, 235 Mo. App. 249, 131 S.W. 2d. 375 (1939).

O'Leary v. Social Security Board, 59 F. Supp. 997 (1945).

Patterson v. Colorado, 205 U.S. 454, 27 S. Ct. 556, 51 L. Ed. 879 (1907).

People v. Alaska Pacific S.S. Co., 182 Cal. 202, 187 P. 742 (1920).

People ex rel. Vollmar v. Stanley, 81 Colo. 276, 255 P. 610 (1927).

People of Illinois v. Levensen, 404 Ill. 574, 90 N.E. 2d. 213 (1950).

Permoldi v. First Municipality No. 1 of New Orleans, 44 U.S. 561, 11 L. Ed. 739 (1845).

Pierce v. Society of Sisters, 268 U.S. 510, 45 S. Ct. 571, 69 L. Ed. 1070 (1925).

Prince v. Massachusetts, 321 U.S. 158, 64 S. Ct. 438, 88 L. Ed. 645 (1945).

Prudential Insurance Co. of America v. Cheek, 259 U.S. 530, 42 S. Ct. 516, 66 L. Ed. 1044 (1922).

Reynolds v. United States, 98 U.S. 145, 25 L. Ed. 244 (1878).

Rice v. Commonwealth, 188 Va. 224, 49 S.E. 2d. 342 (1948).

Richardson v. State, 5 Tex. App. 470 (1880).

St. Patrick's Catholic Church v. Daly, 116 Ill. 76, 4 N.E. 241 (1886).

Santos v. Holy Roman Catholic and Apostolic Church, Philippine, 212 U.S. 463, 29 S. Ct. 338, 53 L. Ed. 599 (1908).

Schlichter v. Keitter, 156 Pa. 119, 27 Atl. 45 (1893).

Schneider v. State, 308 U.S. 147, 60 S. Ct. 146, 84 L. Ed. 155 (1939).

School District of Abington Township v. Schempp, 374 U.S. 203, 83 S. Ct. 1560, 10 L. Ed. 2d. 844 (1963).

Scott Co. v. Roman Catholic Archbishop, Diocese of Oregon, 83 Or. 97, 163 P. 88 (1917).

Searle v. Roman Catholic Bishop of Springfield, 203 Mass. 493, 89 N.E. 809 (1909).

Shannon v. Frost, 42 Ky. 253 (1842).

Sherbert v. Verner, 374 U.S. 398, 83 S. Ct. 1790, 10 L. Ed. 2d. 965 (1963).

Smith v. Bonhovf, 2 Mich. 115 (1851).

Smith v. Donahue, 202 N. Y. App. Div. 656, 195 N. Y. Supp. 715 (1922).

Sneed v. Tippett, 114 Okla. 173, 245 P. 40 (1926).

State v. Board of Trustees, 175 Mo. 52, 74 S.W. 990 (1903).

State v. Cosgrove, 36 Idaho 278, 210 P. 393 (1922).

State v. Matheny, 122 S.C. 459, 101 S.E. 666 (1919).

State v. Peterman, 32 Ind. App. 665, 70 N.E. 550 (1904).

State v. Pilkington, 310 S.W. 2d. 304 (1958).

State v. Will, 99 Kan. 167, 160 P. 1025 (1916).

State v. Wright, 41 Ark. 410, 48 Am. Rep. 43 (1883).

State ex rel. Soares v. Hebrew Congregation, 31 La. App. 205, 33 Am. Rep. 217 (1879).

Stephens v. Bongart, 15 N.J. Misc. 80, 189 Atl. 131 (1937).

Swart v. South Burlington, 122 Vt. 177, 167 Atl. 2d. 514 (1961).

Terminiello v. City of Chicago, 337 U.S. 1, 69 S. Ct. 894, 93 L. Ed. 1131 (1949).

Thomas v. Collins, 323 U.S. 516, 65 S. Ct. 315, 89 L. Ed. 430 (1945).

Thornhill v. Alabama, 310 U.S. 88, 60 S. Ct. 736, 84 L. Ed. 1093 (1940).

Torcaso v. Watkins, 367 U.S. 488, 81 S. Ct. 1680, 6 L. Ed. 2d. 982 (1961).

Tucker v. Texas, 326 U. S. 517, 66 S. Ct. 274, 90 L. Ed. 274 (1945).

United States v. Ballard, 322 U.S. 78, 64 S. Ct. 882, 88 L. Ed. 1148 (1944).

United States v. Cruikshank, 92 U.S. 542, 23 L. Ed. 588 (1875).

Veselka v. Flores, 283 S.W. 303 (1926).

Watchtower Bible and Tract Society v. Metropolitan Life Insurance Company, 297 N.Y. 339, 79 N.E. 2d. 433 (1948); cert. denied 335 U.S. 886, 69 S. Ct. 432, 93 L. Ed. 425 (1948).

Watson v. Avery, 65 Ky. 332 (1867).

Watson v. Jones, 80 U.S. 679, 20 L. Ed. 666 (1871).

West Virginia State Board of Education v. Barnett, 319 U.S. 624, 63 S. Ct. 1178, 87 L. Ed. 1628 (1943).

Zorach v. Clauson, 343 U.S. 306, 72 S. Ct. 679, 96 L. Ed. 954 (1952).

INDEX OF ABBREVIATIONS

AAS—Acta Apostolicae Sedis
Ala.—Alabama Reports
Ala. App.—Alabama Appeals
Am. Rep.—American Reports
App. D.C.—United States Appeals, Circuit Courts of Appeals, District of Columbia
Ark.—Arkansas Reports
ASS—Acta Sanctae Sedis
Atl.—Atlantic Reporter
Atl. 2d.—Atlantic Reporter, Second Series
Atl. Sup. 2d.—Atlantic Supplement, Second Series
Cal.—California Reports
Colo.—Colorado Reports
F. Supp.—Federal Supplement
Ill.—Illinois Reports
Ind. App.—Indiana Appeals
Kan.—Kansas Reports
Ky.—Kentucky Reports
La. App.—Louisiana Appeals
L. Ed.—Lawyers' Edition United States Supreme Courts Reports
L. Ed. 2d.—Lawyers' Edition United States Supreme Court Reports, Second Series
Mass.—Massachusetts Reports
Md.—Maryland Reports
Me.—Maine Reports
Miss.—Mississippi Reports
Mo.—Missouri Reports
Mo. App.—Missouri Appeals
N.E.—Northeastern Reporter
N.E. 2d.—Northeastern Reporter, Second Series
Neb.—Nebraska Reports
N.H.—New Hampshire Reports
N.J. Eq.—New Jersey Court of Equity
N.J.L.—New Jersey Law Reports
N.J. Misc.—New Jersey Miscellaneous
N.W.—Northwestern Reporter
N.Y.—New York Reports
N.Y. App. Div.—New York Appellate Division
N.Y. Sup.—New York Supplement
Ohio—Ohio Reports

Ore.—Oregon Reports
P.—Pacific Reporter
Pa.—Pennsylvania Reports
P. 2d.—Pacific Reporter, Second Series
Pa. Sup.—Pennsylvania Superior
S.C.—South Carolina Reports
S. Ct.—Supreme Court Reporter of Decisions of United States Supreme Court
S.E.—Southeastern Reporter
S.E. 2d.—Southeastern Reporter, Second Series
So.—Southern Reporter
S.W.—Southwestern Reporter
S.W. 2d.—Southwestern Reporter, Second Series
Tenn.—Tennessee Reports
Tex. App.—Texas Appeals
Tex. Crim.—Texas Criminal
U.S.—United States Reports Cases Adjudged in the Supreme Court
Va.—Virginia Reports
Vt.—Vermont Reports

BIOGRAPHICAL NOTE

Thomas F Donovan was born on November 5, 1930, in Brooklyn, New York. He received his elementary education at Our Lady of Perpetual Help School, Richmond Hill, New York. He attended Bishop Loughlin Memorial High School, graduating from that institution in January, 1949. After attending Saint Francis College, Brooklyn, New York, he entered the Seminary of the Immaculate Conception, located in Huntington, New York. He was ordained June 1, 1957, for the Diocese of Brooklyn, New York. After serving as an assistant pastor in two parishes, he enrolled in the fall of 1962 in the School of Canon Law at the Catholic University of America. He received the degree of the Baccalaureate in Canon Law in June, 1963, and that of the Licentiate in June, 1964.

CANON LAW STUDIES*

445. Buckley, Rev. John M., O.S.A., J.C.L., The writings of St. Augustine as sources of canon law. (microfilm)

446. Donovan, Rev. Thomas F., J.C.L., The status of the Church in American civil law and canon law.

447. Dougherty, Rev. T. David, J.C.L., The vicar general of the episcopal ordinary.

448. Palma, Rev. Feliciano M., B.A., J.C.L., A comparative study of wills in canon law and in the civil code of the Philippines. (microfilm)

*For a complete list of the available numbers of this series apply to the Catholic University of America Press, 620 Michigan Avenue, N.E., Washington, D. C. 20017, for a general catalogue.

ALPHABETICAL INDEX

www.ingramcontent.com/pod-product-compliance
Lightning Source LLC
LaVergne TN
LVHW050218080826
844660LV00012B/430

* 9 7 8 0 8 1 3 2 2 6 2 2 4 *